NO ORDINARY
HOME

NO ORDINARY HOME

CAROL JO BRAZO

MULTNOMAH BOOKS · SISTERS, OREGON

NO ORDINARY HOME

published by Multnomah Books
a part of the Questar publishing family

© 1995 by Carol Jo Brazo

International Standard Book Number: 0-88070-744-5

Cover illustration by Hilber Nelson

Printed in the United States of America

Scripture quotations are from:
The Holy Bible, New International Version (NIV)
© 1973, 1984 by International Bible Society,
used by permission of Zondervan Publishing House

For information:
Questar Publishers, Inc.
Post Office Box 1720
Sisters, Oregon 97759

95 96 97 98 99 00 01 02 — 10 9 8 7 6 5 4 3 2 1

8:12 PM   Page 1

For Mom, Ruth, Ernestine, Wendy, Karen,
and all the other committee members who graciously taught me well.

And especially for Mark.
You have made husbanding an art form.

C O N T E N T S

Holy at the Heart of Things

Holiness in the Home

Holy Celebrations

Holy Records

Holy at the Heart of Things

*God always
calls unqualified people.*

MADELEINE L'ENGLE

CHAPTER ONE

HELP!

May 1988

I am a lousy mom. I always visualized myself at 120 pounds, every hair in place, kneeling down to sing "Do Re Mi" to three attentive, adoring children in a setting not unlike the Swiss Alps. Instead I am in sweats, fifty pounds overweight, standing in the middle of a busy kitchen with Rachael showing me she has removed her diaper and desecrated my kitchen floor. My kitchen floor of all places. Mr. Clean should be able to eat off of it, and instead...well, never mind.

I feel so inadequate. When did the rosy glow vanish and reality set in? Was it those first sleepless nights that caused me to view my world as less than ideal? Maybe it was the second pregnancy that cast the shadow of exhaustion over my face. I watch other mothers handle their children with seeming ease. Am I the only one who still finds herself saying, "Because I said so!"?

Lord, You know I am a lousy mom. Remember how I yelled at Megan the first time she ate the dog's food? I really yelled, Lord. I didn't calmly explain to her the nutritional elements lacking in Rugby's food. No. I yelled, and at a pitch designed to shatter glass, not to correct an inquisitive child.

I remember the time Rachael hid my car keys and then couldn't find them again. I didn't make it a good game of hide-and-seek while I sang, "These are a few of my favorite things." In shame I admit I was tired and frustrated and late to a meeting, so I yelled at Rachael and stood her in the corner and ransacked the house. By the time I found the keys—at bath time, in the bath tub—the guilt of my anger caused me to add tears to the bubble bath. Thank goodness Rachael is like Jesus. She forgives easily.

I lack wisdom. Megan is a very sensitive child, and yet I fail to take it into consideration, like that day at McDonald's.

"No Mommy. I don't have to. I do my way," two-year-old Megan boasted.

Instead of dealing with her directly, I tried to tease her out of it. "Megan won't be nice to Mommy. Megan won't be Mommy's friend. What will Mommy do?" I cried, resting my head on Rachael's tiny shoulder.

Megan's face crumpled as she sobbed out that she loved me and that "we be friends, Mommy." Weeks later she was still telling Rachael that "we must not hurt Mommy's feelings." You would think I would have learned my lesson. I didn't.

Months later I told Megan's Sunday School class the story of the good Samaritan— apparently too vividly for her. She burst into tears and was inconsolable that anyone would be mean to the poor man on the donkey. I cried along with Megan. I made a mistake. Again.

You see, God, I am just not ready to be a mom. I need to be calmer, more reflective, more sensitive, more loving. I need to be like Mother Teresa.

Instead I am Carol. I get tired, frustrated, angry. I make bad decisions. I lose my keys all the time, without Rachael's help. I tease too much.

God, why did You, in all your knowledge, make me a mom?

Several months ago I ran across my journals from the years when the children were babies. I laughed and cried as I read the ravings of a marginally sane writer and the tender replies of her Lord.

Every spiritual transformation begins with a sincere cry for help. This book is the story of how the gentle Savior responded to my cry and graciously came and changed a disaster area into a sanctuary fit for His dwelling.

Now, before you get all excited and think my house knows no fights, no clutter, no frustration, let me assure you the sanctuary He's creating is still a work in progress. We don't have all the answers. In many ways we're just like most families. In one important way we are not. The King lives at our house, and we have begun to sense His presence. This book is my best attempt to be honest about how we got from there to here.

Because I believe journaling is a profound act and a powerful tool, each chapter will contain entries from my own journals. Writing in a journal chronicles where a person has been and allows the Spirit of God to sort things out on paper and begin to speak. A journal can also serve as a compass to get back on course when you get off track.

Perhaps there is no greater subject for a personal journal than the forging of a home and family, and this is the story of my family. But even more, it's a story of process.

I can't tell you there are magic formulas for turning an ordinary home into a sanctuary. But I can tell you what I know of God and what I know of myself…and how He came to me in my need and transformed my ordinary and sometimes frustrating home into a holy place. God heard my desperate cry and was quick to answer. He came and brought the holy to our house. Here's how it happened.

My husband, Mark, and I began parenting in chaos. Our problems with fertility revolved around my amazing ability to get pregnant: We had three babies in just under three years, leaving a life of order and entering the realm of the insane! I felt completely incapable of creating a home during those years.

I left a job I loved and clothes that required dry cleaning (plus a paycheck to cover the dry cleaning) and entered the world of Pampers, Gerber's strained peas, and on-call, twenty-four-hour work shifts. (No paycheck.) What a culture shock!

On the other hand, Megan was my sunshine, Rachael was my love gift from Jesus, and Noah was my beloved caboose. I didn't want to trade my new life. At least, not often.

What I wanted was a Mary Poppins–Maria Von Trapp type of existence. I wanted beautiful children, a lovely home, gourmet food, and a cultured two-year-old. What I got is reflected in the next two journal entries.

November 1988

Dear God, I come to you a tired, ugly mess. My life is completely out of control. You know I want this home to be a reflection of you. Right now it reflects the chaos before creation. I am so angry and so unhappy. What should I do?

You know it was hard to leave my job. I really felt fulfilled in the classroom. Now I'm here with three small babies and I'm a complete failure. Everyone says I should not even miss my job. MISS IT? You know I cry daily from wanting it back. I've never felt so homesick and been at home! Someone suggested to me that I get professional help—a psychologist. Do I really need a shrink because I have a newborn, a twenty-month-old, and a two-year-old, yet I still miss my job? Wouldn't any thinking person miss her job?

Today Becky called. Her children are grown; her walk with you is enviable. And so I unloaded. I sobbed. I wanted help. Her answer, phrased sweetly, was a reprimand. If I could be home with these children and not find it a fulfilling experience, then I lacked creativity and style.

Creativity and style? Lord, you know I was the Queen of Creativity in my classroom. Style I may never have again, but creativity? I am having trouble being creative right now. Right now creativity is surviving two children in diapers, another who is newly potty trained, running an in-home business, and overseeing a children's ministry.

You're silent, Lord. Won't you speak? I'm done ranting and raving. I'm aware that somewhere I've completely missed your voice. I'm sorry, Lord. Forgive me.

I used to love Rilke's writings. Now they're a chastisement. He admonishes, "If your everyday life seems poor, don't blame it; blame yourself; admit to yourself that you are not enough of a poet to call forth its riches; because for the creator, there is no poverty and no indifferent place."[1]

Lord, you are my creator. For you there is no poor, indifferent place. Somewhere I have missed your will. I am in a poor, impoverished place where there is little beauty of spirit, little music, color, or grace. I want so much for my home to reflect you. I want this to be a tiny taste of the eternal. I would do anything to achieve it.

Please, Jesus. Please come and make this a holy place. Bring the holy home to my house.

May 1989

Today there will be five children at my home in addition to the three we own. No one is over five years old. Eight children under five, and I am utterly and painfully alone with this little tribe—and terrified.

God, do you remember when I used to teach? The kids were seventeen and eighteen years old, and the task was understanding Our Town or Hamlet. We acted things out. We discussed the view each writer held of life. We laughed together. We left energized.

I know I must sound like a broken record. I want so much to be a good servant. I wish I were made like Mary Poppins, but let's face it, God, you goofed with me.

I need to be honest, even if the kids read this journal someday. I miss Mark as a lover. Now he's the other half of a survival team. No more late, loving mornings in bed. Now we push at each other to establish who has to get up and take care of a child. No more candlelight dinners with soft music and hands stretched out over the linen tablecloth in an embrace. Now we both work as hard as we can to get all three children bathed, fed, loved, and read to. Then the Olympic challenge: Can we get all three to sleep at the same time?

Romance after all that? We're lucky to nod a smile in each other's direction before we collapse on opposite couches.

But I do remember. I remember teaching with Mark; he taught physics and I taught honors English. We ate lunch together, went to live theater, saw movies before they came out on video. We ate at places that required silverware. Writing the bills was not a balancing act, let alone a time to mourn.

Mark and I attended church together and sat through entire services without interruption. We sat before the Savior's feet, as Mary did, and worshiped. Now I frequently wonder why we bother to go. Neither one of us is ever in the entire service.

We used to ski, leaving school on Friday afternoons to head gleefully to the mountains. I can still close my eyes and remember the rush of hooking my boots into the ski bindings and shoving off. Unbelievable fun!

I love my children, Lord. They are the eighth wonder of the world. I look at them and am awestruck by your creation. I would not trade them for anything.

It's just that I miss grown-up fun. I miss the intellectual exchanges. I miss attending church and knowing I have really worshiped. I miss talking to Mark until we run out of things to say, instead of until one of us falls asleep.

I feel a bit imprisoned and guilty for saying so. But I've read prison literature. You do some of your best work in prisons. Prisons are wonderful settings for your special magic, God. The darker the backdrop, the brighter the light.

O God, teach me to bless my prison. Will you reveal it to me for what it truly is? Is it a sanctuary? Is the prison just a disguise?

Before I knew it, the chase was on. The goal? Try to find the sanctuary hidden in the prison walls. I needed to see my world, my work, and myself through new eyes. It called for vulnerability. It also called for faith. And the first move was all mine.

Jesus says, "You will know the truth and the truth will set you free." The truth was that I needed help, and no matter how wonderful my own mother was, there was only One who could help me. I needed my Savior.

I turned to Scripture and found these words: "In my distress I called to the LORD; I cried to my God for help. From his temple he heard my voice; my cry came before him, into his ears" (Psalm 18:6).

Right then I laid my heart bare before Him. I told Him of my failures—all of them. I told Him of all my desires. Anyone could see that the reality of my life and the desires of my heart were light-worlds apart.

I returned to the psalms. They were rich in hope and promises. "O LORD my God, I called to you for help and you healed me" (Psalm 30:2). "The righteous cry out, and the LORD hears them; he delivers them from all their troubles. The LORD is close to the brokenhearted and saves those who are crushed in spirit" (Psalm 34:17-18).

Parenthood is a tightrope walk on which we balance precariously between the vulnerable joy of watching our children grow and the spirit-crushing despair that fills us when we fail as parents. Here I read a promise that God would deliver me and stay near me as I walked that tightrope.

Psalm 46 reminded me that God is an ever-present help. With three children under three, ever-present was what I needed.

I began to relax inside. Scripture, as always, was working its calm peace into me, reminding me that my help comes from the Lord who made heaven and earth. His credentials for handling the Brazo bunch did seem adequate—*better* than adequate. I cried out for help, and help arrived.

All transformations begin with an acknowledgment of need. If you have children, you have need. None of us are wise enough to parent on our own. Pick up your pen, and take a few minutes to express your own cry for help. Bring the holy home to your house and begin to experience what Christ can do when you put Him at the center of your home. The Creator of the Universe is just waiting for your call.

CHAPTER TWO

WHATEVER HAPPENED TO ME?

January 1, 1989

I sat in front of the mirror today and wondered what happened. Obviously, three children in three years, but a lot more than that must have happened. I don't look like myself at all.

Weight is probably the biggest factor. I must be fifty pounds overweight. There's one sure way to find out. Nah.

Really, I don't think weight is the biggest factor. Neither is the fact that I haven't visited a makeup counter in three years. I think my whole life has changed beyond recognition. All of it. Three babies, no money, no job. Even our church has dissolved. You know, Lord, if I feel like I've landed in someone else's skin, there are reasons. The problem is, I don't know how to change it.

One friend told me that if my job was so important to me, I should go back to work. So what if three-quarters of the salary goes to childcare. I'd have the satisfaction of doing something I love.

Boy, does that make me feel guilty. "Doing something I love." As if I didn't love, adore, and cherish these three wonderful babies. I love them. I love being with them. It's just really hard. Mark is working two jobs to make ends meet and is exhausted all the time. No one talks in complete sentences. No one reads.

We watched a television show the other night, and a woman who had only one baby was at a dinner party. She was trim and looked great. While people were talking around her, she was thinking, "I have nothing to contribute. I have a nine-month-old baby. I am brain dead."

Mark laughed and I cried. It was too close to the truth. I have no idea what's happening in my culture—the latest books, movies, plays. Are they still writing plays?

I don't know if I like the person I'm becoming. I'm bored by women who spend all their time talking about their kids. So, instead of finding friends in the same boat, I'm becoming a hermit. An overweight, under-read hermit.

My first five years with children were the hardest on my self-esteem. I had valued my job, my church, and my marriage so highly that the things I did defined me. I believed that I *was* what I did.

Once the kids arrived, I valued my job as a mother. I believed then and I believe now that motherhood is a high calling. It is a good, noble, and wonderful thing to have children and raise them to be God-loving, independent, creative adults. I just had trouble equating the day-in and day-out mundane chores of housekeeping and child raising with that mystical and holy thing called mothering. I still thought mothering was done on a hill in the Swiss Alps with a guitar on your shoulder and a gourmet picnic at your feet.

The problem was that my self-esteem was tied directly to what I did, not to who I was. Until you settle the issue of your own worth, it's impossible to bring holiness into anyone else's life. Until you understand that your worth is already determined by the fact of your birth, everything else is an exercise in propping up a dying tree.

God began to deal with my sagging sense of self-worth in a most unusual way. He brought a ladder into my house. To this day that ladder is an honored and revered part of our home's decor. Here is the story.

April 1990

Today was a lovely day. Mark took me for a long drive up to my favorite shop in Centralia, Washington. Think of it! A beautiful spring day and no children! What a date.

We took our time, driving at a leisurely pace and lunching at Señor Nelson's, which has the best Mexican food I've ever tasted. We should have shared one entree. We both felt sick we were so full. Served us right for overindulging.

The shop, full of beautiful things, was a delight. I loved the books, the pottery, the art. But at the back of the shop an item caught my eye, and I fell in love with it on sight. A rough pine ladder. I couldn't take my eyes off it. I walked over and just stared at this unfinished piece made of round poles of pine with knots all over it.

When my eyes had drunk their fill, my hands took over. I loved the feel of the silly thing. It was rough and smooth all at the same time. It was stark. My hands caressed and caressed. Mark came by and in typical fashion said, "What is it?"

"Jacob's ladder," I softly replied.

"Jacob's ladder? Why Jacob's ladder?"

"I don't know. I must be crazy. I just love it. Don't you?"

"Sure, Carol. It's a very nice ladder. It's also useless as a ladder, so what would you do with it?" His voice took on a logical tone, true to the science teacher he is.

"I don't have the slightest idea. How much is it?" I countered.

"You're not going to believe this. It's $200!" he exclaimed, his loud whisper filling the room.

"Ummmm."

"Now, Carol, we don't have $200 for a ladder," came his gentle reminder.

"I know, it's just that...never mind."

I slipped my hand into his and enjoyed the sympathetic squeeze. Never mind that the ladder didn't speak to him; he was sorry I couldn't have it.

On the way home Mark suggested I save the money for it. What a guy. I've already figured out how to get the first $25.

July 1990

I am so disappointed. Silly of me. I know better than to get myself worked up about something as crazy as that ladder in Centralia. I can't even explain why I wanted the dumb thing. What a jolt to find it gone!

I saved the money, every dollar secure in my checking account, in time for our overnight stay in Seattle. An anniversary gift to me. Mark, sweet man that he is, was as happy as I that we were off to get Jacob's ladder.

We went to Señor Nelson's and had a feast. We meandered, savoring the time alone and the conquest of the ladder. We finally went into the shop, headed straight for the spot, and...no ladder. Certain that it had to be somewhere, I checked every nook and cranny before asking the clerk.

"No, I'm sorry. It sold immediately. What did you call it? Jacob's ladder?"

"Can you order another one?" I asked, my stomach sinking to my shoes.

"I'm so sorry. It was a special purchase. One of a kind," the clerk replied.

O God, please remove this black cloud hanging over our anniversary. I really want to put this thing behind me. I also wanted that ladder, but as Mark so wisely pointed out, all things work together for my good. All things. Even disappointing shopping sprees.

September 1990

UNBELIEVABLE! Lord, you are absolutely unbelievable. Who would have thought in July that by September there would be an exact replica of my Jacob's ladder in Newberg, Oregon. And the price!

On Labor Day weekend Mom had come to spend a few hours with the children. After an afternoon of "Grandma this" and "Grandma that," even she was ready for a break. Mark watched the kids, and Mom and I hopped into the van.

We stopped at a little cafe for coffee and tea, relaxing and laughing over the antics of the children. Then we decided to check out Hazel's, the new antique and country furnishings store in town.

We walked in, looked at the various goodies, and then we saw it. Right before our eyes was Jacob's ladder. We both rushed to it and grabbed the price tag. Thirty dollars. We smiled— coconspirators. We grabbed that ladder as if it were the last piece of gold on the North American continent. No one loves smart shopping more than my mom, and boy did we feel smart.

It was such fun. Mark saw it come into the house and smiled his lazy smile.

"How much, hon?" he quietly asked.

"Thirty big ones!" I laughed.

"Thirty, huh? Still sad you didn't get it in July?" he teased.

"No. I do remember some wise man telling me that all things worked together for…what was it?…my good? Even ruined shopping trips."

Lord, thank you for my ladder. It rests against the fireplace and is lovely. Honestly, Lord, I still don't know why I'm so drawn to it. My hands just love the feel of it. My eyes fly to it constantly. Maybe it's just a reminder of your care. Of your love for handling the small things in life. Of your giving nature. It's a beautiful representation of those things. Thank you.

June 1991

Tonight we shared our Sabbath with Jack and Linda. Since it was a lovely summer evening, we had dessert outdoors on the deck. Afterwards Jenny and Tom, ages thirteen and eight, taught Megan, Rachael, and Noah, ages five, four, and two, the story of Jacob's ladder. The kids had a sweet time together. Jenny and Tom had drawn pictures to illustrate the story, and our children were mesmerized. It's a special delight to listen to children teach children. Their words take on a profound depth of which they are totally unaware.

The children were excused and romped off in search of toys. The adults began to share their views of Jacob and his life. Jack asked what was the significance of Jacob's ladder in my life. It came to me in a flash.

When Jacob sees the ladder, the Lord is at the top. God says, "I am the LORD, the God of your father Abraham and the God of Isaac. I will give you and your descendants the land on which you are lying.... All peoples on earth will be blessed through you and your offspring. I am with you and will watch over you wherever you go, and I will bring you back to this land. I will not leave you until I have done what I have promised you" (Genesis 28:13-15).

Later in life, Jacob wrestles with God and refuses to let go of Him until God blesses him. In blessing him, God changes his name from Jacob to Israel.

This is what I am asking of God. I'm asking Him to name me, to tell me what is His place for me in His kingdom. I have always thought I was a teacher. Now He has named me wife and mother. That ladder is a sign of my wrestling with God, of my desire to be named and to know what work He has for me to do.

Jacob had been unaware of God's presence prior to the dream. After the dream, he said, "Surely the LORD is in this place, and I was not aware of it." Lord, are you in this place? This home? Am I blind to your face, deaf to your footsteps?

Over the next several weeks I came to understand I had things confused. Mark suggested I look to Scripture to see what God had said about who I was. Sounded like a great place to start.

Romans 8:16-17 says that "we are God's children. Now if we are children, then we are heirs—heirs of God and co-heirs with Christ."

John 1:12 says, "To all who received him, to those who believed in his name, he gave the right to become children of God—children born not of a natural descent, nor of human decision or a husband's will, but born of God."

These two passages, known from childhood, spoke loudly to me. "Born of God." "Heirs of God." "Children of God." There's power in my heritage. I am a child of God. Born of God. Entitled to all that is His. Loved by Him as my children are loved by me. Only, He loves fully, perfectly.

My pulse began to race. If this were true, really true, and the only requirement was my belief...I could only begin to comprehend it. Five years later the words still give me chills, and I still can hardly believe the truth of them.

My children cannot *do* anything to earn my love. They have it—all of it. It was given to them at conception. Just by the reality of their being, they are loved by me. Is it possible the same is true of my relationship with God?

Scripture says it is. But my humanity doubts it. I begin to catalogue my sins, just in case God didn't know what He was getting into with me.

God listens to the list. Patiently. With a smile. Then He sends me back to the written Word.

Colossians 1:13 says, "For he has rescued us from the dominion of darkness and brought us into the kingdom of the Son he loves, in whom we have redemption, the forgiveness of sins."

Okay. I am forgiven. A child of God. Born of God. Forgiven. But my human nature just can't believe it. I must *do* something to earn this. I must do something!

And the childhood verses return—verses committed to memory between the ages of five and ten. They return in Dolby Surround Sound.

"For it is by grace you have been saved, through faith—and this not from yourselves, it is the gift of God—not by works, so that no one can boast. For we are God's workmanship, created in Christ Jesus to do good works, which God prepared in advance for us to do" (Ephesians 2:8-10).

"Therefore, since we have been justified through faith, we have peace with God through our Lord Jesus Christ, through whom we have gained access by faith into this grace in which we now stand" (Romans 5:1-2).

There is nothing I can do. Nothing. I am *His* workmanship. Even the good works I am to do were prepared for me ahead of time. I am justified through faith in *His* redemptive work. No job, no career, no success, no amount of financial reward—*nothing* will ever earn me His approval and love. I already have it.

If there were one biblical truth I wish I could give my children and lay hold of in my own deepest parts, it would be this one thing. He created me, He loves me, He will always love me. Nothing I do will change who I am.

Being versus doing. The error was finally outlined in bold. I was always worried about what I was doing. I was even worried about what Mark was doing and not doing…what my children were doing and not doing.

God's only concern was and is what I am *being*—a child of His, forgiven, justified by the work of His Son, His heir. Being a new creation (2 Corinthians 5:17). Being transformed by a renewed mind (Romans 12:1-2). Being led by the Spirit of God (Romans 8:14). And catch this one, being the righteousness of God (2 Corinthians 5:21). These are the things I am. By the virtue of my faith in Jesus. He did everything that needed doing; I needed to relax and concentrate on being. The only thing I need to *do* is come to grips with God's way of seeing me.

And so, in my deepest places, I rehearse God's Word. Over and over I tell myself the truth. I am His creation. I am His child. I am joint heirs with Christ. And all of this is His gift. I don't need to do anything. I just need to be a child of God, convinced of this fact in my deepest places and converted to His name for me. He calls me "His."

It is finally clear. It was His name that I craved, not a definition of roles. A realization of a name. A holy name.

The ladder became an altar for me. Just as the Israelites built altars out of stone to remind them and their children of the work of God in their lives, the ladder reminds me that God changed my name and rescued me from the dominion of darkness. He took me, claimed me as His own, and gave me His name.

Often someone will visit my home and notice that funny old ladder. Hands reach out and caress it with the same tenderness that mine first did. And the story is usually told again as it was when Bob and Cathy came to visit.

March 1992

This week Bob and Cathy came to visit. The kids had a blast playing in the cold Oregon ocean. Five kids, ages six and under. What a playground; what fun!

It was so good to be with Cathy again. I have missed my college buddies so much the last eleven years. What a joy to have her right here, in my house. We reverted, drinking Coke for breakfast, visiting every antique store in the state, and chattering late into the night. We looked for property for them to retire on someday. We talked till we couldn't stay awake and cried when they drove away.

During that visit, Bob and I had an interesting exchange. Bob had paused before Jacob's ladder and raised an eyebrow as only Bob can do. "Okay, Carol, what is this?" he asked.

"It's Jacob's ladder, Bob."

"Umm. Why Jacob's ladder? What's the point?" he countered.

"Oh, Bob," I moaned. "All the time I've been out of the classroom I've felt I was somehow less important in God's scheme of things. I've felt at loose ends. I kept wanting God to name me and give me a career. This ladder is a message from Him to me. He has named me. He named me 'His Own.' He needs to remind me, every day, that careers are roles, but identity is found in Him. I keep forgetting this, and He's using this ladder to remind me."

"Really? All that from a pine ladder?" Thoughtful eyes found mine.

"There's more. It also reminds me that He is physically present in this house, today. When Jacob woke up from his dream, he said, 'Surely the LORD is in this place, and I was not aware of it.' I see the ladder and am reminded that He is physically here."

Silence. Those intense eyes were somewhere else. Then came the real question. "Isn't that, well, isn't it a bit confrontational? I mean, on a daily basis?"

Lord, I have thought a lot about Bob's words. It is confrontational. It daily confronts my error regarding identity and jobs. But really, Lord, it's comforting too. It tells me you have named me. So even if I'm mopping the kitchen floor AGAIN, or cleaning toilets, or folding clothes, my worth is safe in your sight. My value as a person is secure in you. I am pleasing you. And I want to please you more than anything.

You, reader, also wear many hats—sacred crowns. You're a mother, a daughter, a sister, possibly an employee, a wife, a chauffeur, a parent-helper in the schools, a Sunday School teacher, a VBS coordinator. Frankly, the list seems endless. Each of these roles is important; each has sacred responsibilities. But not one of them defines us. Not one!

Who we are is the question; what we do is not the answer. Let's examine Scripture and find the answers to what defines us.

1. Look up each passage of Scripture below and write what it tells you about who you really are.

John 1:12-13 _recieve + believe → children of God, born of God_

John 3:18 _God's one + only Son, Jesus_

Psalm 139:13 _He knit me together_

Psalm 139:14 _His work → fearfully + wonderfully made_

Psalm 139:16 _Saw my unformed body, ordained my days_

Romans 8:16-17 _Heirs of God, co-heirs w/ Christ_

Colossians 1:13 _subjects of the kingdom of the Son_

Ephesians 2:8-10 _Salvation by grace + faith — Not works_
God's workmanship

2 Corinthians 5:17 _New creation_

Romans 12:1 _Living sacrifice_

2 Corinthians 5:21 _In Christ I am the righteousness of God_

2. Take two of those passages you find the hardest to believe in your own heart and rehearse them. Memorize them. Say them daily, hourly, until your very bones begin to sense the truth of God's Word.

3. List three changes that would take place in your life if you really believed these Scriptures.

Being would be of greater importance than doing.

4. Now, commit to being an aware child of the Most High. Take His name consciously for your own. Work hard to believe what He knows to be the truth. Read the following letter and commit your work to your Father.

DEAREST LORD,

How can I possibly thank you? I have read your analysis of who I am. I have to tell you, this looks too good to be true.

It will take me awhile to get used to all of this. But believe me, I will try. I will rehearse your truth in my heart and mind until I know the reality of it. This week I will begin with these two truths:

wonderfully made and _your rightousness_ .

Thank you. Who but you could see me this way?

CHAPTER THREE

HOLY MYSTERY

May 9, 1983

Last night Mark asked me to marry him.

On Friday he had wired me sixteen long-stemmed yellow roses with a note that read, "Dearest Carol, you are the sunshine of my life. All my love, Mark."

Saturday I worked at the restaurant until 1:00 a.m. and then drove home to see the flowers. I sat admiring them as I flipped through the mail. Alas, nothing from Mark. There was, however, something from Western Union. Being the organized person I am, I got depressed thinking I had failed to pay a bill and some company was desperately trying to collect its twenty dollars. I decided to open it later.

I fiddled, and finally headed to bed. Once there, sleep was impossible. I was bothered by that Western Union thing. I got up and went back to the kitchen table. I opened the telegram, read it, digested it. Then I reread it. And read it again—twenty or thirty times—until I had memorized it. It read, "Dear Carol, I love you. I adore you. I cherish you. I want to marry you. Will you marry me? Love, Mark."

I sat down on the kitchen floor, ignoring the chairs, and hugged my knees to my chest like a little girl. Shock settled in. The thing I wanted most in the whole wide world had happened. Mark wanted to marry me.

I reviewed the reasons why I was confident this was the will of the Lord. I tried to think of any reservations I might have. Then I retreated back into the comfort of shock.

Twenty minutes later I realized a reply was customary. I pondered how to do it right. Should I take time and be creative? Nah. I wanted to tell him right that minute. I dialed his number.

Once I was sure he was awake, I told him I had received a telegram and had just one question—"When?"

Mark, with a smile in his voice, said, "No yes or no, just 'when'?"

"Yes, yes, a thousand times yes!" I cried.

That night we planned our future while wrapped in a fog of bliss. We laughed. I cried. We smiled. Most important, we prayed. We asked God to bless our home. To bless our marriage with boundless love. To use our marriage to His glory. We gave thanks.

In 1983 Mark and I covenanted to explore the mystery of marriage, to seek for the rest of our lives to understand the puzzle of oneness—the picture of Christ and His Church.

Marriage is at the heart of our lives as women, whether we are single or married. Isaiah 54:5-6 tells us: "'For your Maker is your husband—the LORD Almighty is his name—the Holy One of Israel is your Redeemer; he is called the God of all the earth. The LORD will call you back as if you were a wife deserted and distressed in spirit—a wife who married young, only to be rejected,' says your God."

It doesn't matter, in the realm of the eternal, if we have earthly husbands or not. Single parents are promised that God Himself will take on that role. He will husband them. He will manage them and their affairs. He will provide for them.

So when we look at marriage, there are lessons for those who are married and for those who parent alone. We are each called to build a holy place, a home. We are each called to recognize the marriage union and to work hard to understand it and flourish in it.

Marriage on earth is a pattern of the marriage of Christ and His Church. We live in marriage to understand the lessons of the eternal. We are rehearsing eternity. Whether our bridegroom is an earthly brother the Lord has brought into our lives to teach us about our Eternal Bridegroom or our bridegroom is the Lord God Almighty Himself, we are husbanded.

And so we are left to ask, How do I bring the holy into my marriage? How can that relationship become a holy haven? A protected place?

I found the image of an enclosed garden to be most important for me. I had seen lush and gorgeous walled gardens, which were made for just one purpose—to provide a place of refuge and beauty for the owner. That picture, found in the Song of Songs, was what Mark and I used to build our marriage.

The first thing we found was that we needed to build secure boundaries into our relationship. Enclosed gardens have walls that keep them set apart from the rest of the world. We needed "walls" (found in God's Word) that would keep thieves out and give the garden of our marriage a protected environment in which to grow and bloom.

Whether you have an earthly husband or not, your relationship with Jesus also needs to have a secure wall that will keep thieves away but will allow a safe blooming of your relationship with Him.

The first section of wall for our garden was formed by Genesis 2:23-25, a pure commandment. It was set up prior to mankind's Fall and was what God intended prior to the curse. It reads, "The man said, 'This is now bone of my bones and flesh of my flesh; she shall be called "woman," for she was taken out of man.' For this reason a man will leave his father and mother and be united to his wife, and they will become one flesh. The man and his wife were both naked, and they felt no shame."

This first boundary meant that no one would ever come between us. So far, our deepest relationships had been with our families, but God told us to leave them and be one. Now our first loyalty would be to each other. Always. No matter what.

And so we began to pray. We rehearsed these words. We memorized them and asked God to help us live them out. It wasn't always easy.

If you were not blessed with a wonderful childhood and adolescence, you may have had reasons to leave—to grow and start somewhere else. But if everything was provided for your growth within your family of origin, you may have found it harder to step out of that comfort and forge a new home.

Mark and I both love our families deeply. They also love us. God was not asking us to leave them completely, never to see them again. God was asking us to leave home emotionally and spiritually. To look to each other. To decide things together. And God was asking our families, who knew more and could guide clearly, to step back. To quiet their hearts and allow God to work His good pleasure in us.

This boundary was and still is a place of tender consideration. We prune it carefully, guard it gently, and open the gate to our parents' advice regularly. We are blessed. They stand outside the gate and await their invitation. But if they did not wait, if they felt free to crash the gate, we would gently stop them. It is a boundary set by God to be honored.

The second section of wall concerns honoring each other. We compete for each other's affection, trying consistently to inject new intimacies into the marriage. Dennis Rainey of Family Life Ministries says that if we do not compete for our spouse's affection every single day, someone or something else will. This I firmly believe.

31

Honoring means different things at different times. Webster's says honoring is "to respect greatly, to show high regard for, integrity, chastity." In Ephesians the husband is told to love his wife and the wife is told to respect her husband.

My father is fond of saying that if men loved their wives and daughters as Christ loved the Church, the issue of women's place in the world and church would never come up. It would be handled on a basis of love and honor. Because I have a father who loves in that vein, and a husband who works hard to love and honor as Christ would, I am inclined to agree with Dad. When we are loved as Christ loves, we are encouraged, honored, respected, cherished, adored, challenged, and educated, and sacrifices are willingly made for us.

The strident voices clamoring for rights are stilled by genuine love. Genuine love seeks what is best for the other. It serves. It lays down its life for the good of the other. Who can be shrill in the face of true love?

Likewise, oppression is ended by true love. One cannot love as Christ loved and fail to support, encourage, and challenge the loved one. We are all safe in the love of Christ. That love embraces and nourishes and brings about a pure and unsoiled bride who laughs at the future, secure in the love of her bridegroom.

The difficulty is that we are fallen. Not every husband strives to love as Christ loves. Not every wife strives to respect her earthly husband as she does her heavenly Lord. But that is the command. We are to strive for that respect, no matter what.

I learned one of the most profound lessons of my life from my sister's marriage. She lived with a man who did not love her as Christ loved the Church. By his affairs he was actively destroying the sister I loved.

One day I asked her, "Do you still love him?" Her reply shakes me to the bone to this day.

"Carol, I am not responsible for feeling love toward him. I am responsible to act in love toward him. I will act in ways that honor God and leave the emotions up to Him."

She was twenty-four years old at the time. God did not keep her in that relationship much longer. But while she stayed, she worked diligently to love as Christ would love. Taught by our parents, she honored even in the face of abuse. I've never been prouder of her. I don't know if I could do as she did. She represented Jesus to all of us.

Mark and I have learned to honor on much easier ground. One lesson we learned this year was a repeat. Early in our marriage we honored our relationship with frequent dates. Even when the children were babies, we found the money to go to a cheap movie or a picnic concert in the park.

This year my business provided us with some extra money. I was so anxious to get things done on the house. We painted, bought a dining room table, covered some pillows. It may not sound like much, but it was major for us. I was pleased with the house.

However, I was surprised at my feelings toward Mark. Here I was doing all this stuff to the house, and I was getting less and less of his time. Granted, this was not an easy year to teach in Oregon. Contract negotiations and lack of state funds made his life miserable. We spent little time together.

In June we realized we had not had a real date in five months. The last date had been pretty spectacular, but five months without another one? What happened?

The Lord revealed it to me when I cashed my paycheck. I had honored Him with my tithe; I had honored the kids with some money for next year's school clothes; I had honored the house with a new table; I had even honored myself with a new outfit and haircut.

But I had not honored Mark. I had not honored our marriage. I had not set aside any date money, unwilling to save it myself. I was waiting for Mark, who was stressed and in need of some tender loving care. Mark, who works so hard for us. I honored everyone but him.

I repented. I apologized to Mark, to God, and to myself. Then Mark and I had a heart-to-heart talk about my money. You see, Mark has always paid for everything. Any money I earn pays for Christmas, birthdays, school clothes, and furniture. Mark gently told me that he'd rather spend that money on nights out and family outings with the kids than fixing up a kitchen. He was right. The kitchen would always be there, but these days with Mark and the kids would not. The house needed to move down on my list of priorities.

The third section of boundaries we built had to do with being one. Scripture tells us that the two shall become one. Our prayer at the time of our engagement was that the Lord would give us one heart. We covenanted with God that we would not move in any direction if we did not have one heart. One heart was and is our guideline for decision making.

This boundary is undergirded with Scripture. Each decision-making move of the gate requires a trip to Scripture to make sure we are in tune. No, we do not always get it straight. We often make mistakes. And sometimes we rush through the gate together only to find the Savior has not followed. But God is gracious. We seldom rush out without Him. And when we do, He comes when we finally cry out for help.

The fourth gate we guard is intimacy. Proverbs 4:23 instructs us to "guard your heart, for it is the wellspring of life." Genesis 2 tells us a man will be united, or will cleave, to his wife. Except for the lordship of Jesus Christ, no one comes close to the place of my husband in my life. I guard this. I treasure this.

Mark and I have built this boundary with joy. We share our deepest thoughts and hopes with each other. I may share some with close female friends, but I share everything with Mark.

Intimacy in the physical part of our relationship has been a joy for both of us. I was blessed during the last days of our engagement to have a circle of older, married, female friends who took it upon themselves to give me an education. They laughingly taught of the fun that married intimacy provides. They spoke openly and frankly about the importance of keeping play in the marriage. They gave me suggestions, sharing with tender smiles and dancing eyes the importance of a good love life.

This education was important. As Christians we concentrate a great deal on sexual purity. This is important; virginity is to be highly prized. But new brides need different lessons. They need to know that now, in the holy state of matrimony, there is purity in play. Sex can be a lighthearted joy as well as a profound sharing of two souls. I took the lessons to heart and Mark agreed they were lessons he approved of—body and soul!

As our marriage grew, babies came on the scene. It was time then to learn about seasons in intimacy—seasons of change and seasons of drought. This lesson was not a lot of fun. It was filled with guilt. I felt guilty that I was often too tired to do more than wave at Mark. It helped me a great deal to be with other young mothers—tired, worn out, uninterested young mothers.

February 1987

I have been missing Bible Study Fellowship. With the new baby I felt it necessary to drop out for this year. The lecturer is a wonderful woman named Pat—forty, well dressed (no oatmeal on her clothes), well read, and articulate. I love listening to this woman teach. Nancy heard me moan about it again and offered to drop by after class and tell me a few gems...a few revelations from Scripture...to brighten my day with a few great quotes.

I was broke, so I ran to the grocery store and turned in pop cans, enough for a hamburger and a Coke. Nancy shared her French fries. We got the kids settled, and then Nancy leaned forward conspiratorially.

"You'll never believe what one woman said in class today," she said, a smile in her voice.

"Ummm…what?" I asked, handing Megan a dish of Cheerios.

"Well, she came into class clearly exhausted. She plopped down in a chair, stretched out her legs, and groaned. Then she eyed each one of us and said, 'I feel like a jungle gym! My kids climb all over me all day long, and then my husband is all over me at night!'"

I looked up, shocked. Giggles turned into a roar of laughter.

"I can't believe she said that! What did everyone do?"

"Just what we did. They laughed till they cried," Nancy finished.

I've been thinking a lot about that line. I mean, Mark is not all over me. And I am certainly not all over him. It's just that I've been holding or touching or carrying someone all day long. When he comes home, I want him to hold and carry the kids and leave me alone. It isn't that I don't love the man. I adore him. It's just that I've been spit up on, wet on, gurgled on, and there is still cereal on the kitchen floor. Who feels like romance after all that?

While I'm not a biblical scholar, the Song of Songs gave me great comfort during those days. In chapter 5 the beloved is awakened by her lover. She is clearly not anxious to get up and open the door for him. Her response is not unlike mine: "I have taken off my robe—must I put it on again? I have washed my feet—must I soil them again?" The problem comes when the lover leaves. She has to search for him. It's a clear warning to me: Don't let intimacy wait too long.

Physical intimacy during the year following a baby's birth is not easy for most couples. Exhaustion plays a major role. So does the lack of time and money. Talk about it prior to the baby's arrival. Plan for it. And rest assured, when the baby gets a little older, you'll seek out your lover more regularly. Your desire will return.

Know that all marriages have seasons to them. Seasons of intense intimacy and seasons of drought. Sensitivity and nonsexual expressions of love can go a long way toward reassuring your spouse. And reassurance is usually all anyone needs.

The fifth and final section of our boundary is mystery. Proverbs 30:18-19 confirms this section of our fence. "There are three things that are too amazing for me, four that I do not understand: the way of an eagle in the sky; the way of a snake on a rock; the way of a ship on the high seas; and the way of a man with a maiden."

All of literature confirms that the relationship between husband and wife is a mystery. Men consider women the greatest of all mysteries, and women confirm that no one can really understand men.

We delight in the mystery. It's amazing that you can live with someone for ten years, sharing intimately, living consciously, and still find great depths in that person that are unknown to you.

In Scripture, Esther is a woman who knew how to maintain mystery. She did not spill out her heart when the king asked for her request, not even when he offered her half of his kingdom. No, she calmly invited him and her enemy to a banquet. Even at the banquet she maintained her secret. It was only on the second night of feasting that she finally divulged her request.

This was not a matter of coyness. It was knowing when to state her case. It was taking care of all the king's needs prior to asking for her own. Esther is in Scripture for a reason. Not only was she a powerful woman who saved a nation, she was a woman who knew how to maintain the interest and devotion of her husband. She understood mystery.

Mystery envelopes our marriage. Mark and I have a language all our own designed to state our needs to each other in public without revealing them to the rest of the world. Early in our marriage we found ourselves in social situations where we unconsciously caused each other hurt. To keep this from happening again, we developed a vocabulary that sounds perfectly reasonable to a stranger but conveys a deeper meaning to us. They are code words that mean everything from "You're not listening to me" to "I want you all alone! Let's get out of here!" They are flirtatious, fun, and incredibly useful.

G. K. Chesterton, the theologian, said, "As long as you have mystery, you have health; when you destroy mystery you create morbidity."[1] Healthy marriages remain something of a closed door to others. They are one. How can two be one? Ah...another mystery of Scripture.

Job says, "Can you fathom the mysteries of God? Can you probe the limits of the Almighty? They are higher than the heavens—what can you do? They are deeper than the depths of the grave—what can you know?" (Job 11:7-8).

Romans 16:25 tells us that Jesus is the revelation of the mystery hidden in ages past.

First Timothy 3:16 says, "Beyond all question, the mystery of godliness is great...."

Mystery surrounds the Lord we serve. Mystery surrounds His commands. Mystery surrounds the way of a man with a maiden.

In our society we want to understand everything rationally. It isn't possible. Don't allow society to rob your marriage relationship of mystery. How do two become one? Can you explain it?

Take the next few days to think about your marriage relationship. What boundaries have you built? What boundaries need to be built? Regardless of your married state, ponder what boundaries surround your walk with Jesus. What guards your relationship with Him?

1. Below are several Scripture passages that suggest boundaries. Read them. Ponder them. Ask the Spirit of God to reveal to you the boundaries your marriage relationship needs. Review the walls; what needs mending?

Genesis 2:24

Genesis 2:25

Proverbs 31:11

Ephesians 5:22

Ephesians 5:25

Ephesians 5:32

Hebrews 13:4

Song of Songs 8:14

2. List the boundaries you have in place:

3. List the boundaries you feel the Spirit of God is calling you to build:

4. In what area does your marriage feel unprotected?

5. Isaiah 54:5 tells us "God, your Maker, is your husband." He is capable of protecting you in the areas in which you feel insecure. How have you seen Him protect you?

6. No one is perfectly fulfilled in an earthly marriage relationship; only God is capable of meeting every need. Spend time in prayer thanking God for all the ways He has husbanded you.

Holiness in the Home

✦

Their life was all one piece.
It was all sacred and all ordinary.

SUE BENDER

CHAPTER FOUR

THE DAILIES

February 1987

I need to know where to go to resign. I'm finished as a mother. I cannot possibly continue. I quit.

I have not had a solid night's sleep in decades. I can't find the phone book, and I have a nagging feeling I probably couldn't find the phone if I had to. This house is a disaster!

Mark and the girls would be better off without me. Honestly. I look out my window and can visualize myself, suitcase in hand, trudging down the street. Tears flood my cheeks. My shoulders are slumped in defeat. I turn my head to catch one more glimpse of my husband and children and then shuffle off to bag-lady heaven.

Mark and the girls heave sighs of relief. They quickly organize the mess I've left behind. Everything suddenly has a place, and the house works like clockwork.

Back here in the real world, I'm out of diapers, out of baby food, out of Diet Coke, and out of sorts. Why is it that nothing ever runs smoothly around this house? What does it take to make it a home instead of a demolition derby? Obviously, whatever it takes, I don't have it. I quit. Do you hear that, world? I, Carol Jo Brazo, QUIT!

      I feel fairly confident that those words, penned seven years ago, express the emotions many of us endure. I'll never forget the first time I cried on an older woman's shoulder and told her I was certain that my family would be better off without me. She hushed me and said, "Listen, Carol, every mother feels that way! Most of us think of quitting once a week. You're all right. You're just tired."

I was all right. I was just tired. I was also running a household with no conscious plan of attack. I did everything according to urgency. With children at the ages of two and fourteen months, urgency was all that mattered.

During those difficult days I began to beg God to send help. I was thinking of a nanny, housekeeper, and cook. In that order. God heard my cry and sent a committee. Okay, I know the old saying, "For God so loved the world that He did not send a committee." In my case I needed a committee—a committee of women to teach me the finer parts of running a home.

My committee was made up of people who did not know each other. They simply saw my need and were too kind to pass by on the other side of the street. They fulfilled the section of Scripture in Titus that exhorts older women to teach the younger women.

I was raised by very loving parents. My father, having grown up during the depression, was adamant that his daughters have a leisurely childhood. That meant we did little in the way of household chores. Emphasis on *little.* I made my bed and kept a pathway to it clean. Periodically I mopped the kitchen floor. I did not cook, clean, or iron. Mom ran a beautiful home, an immaculate home (as long as the kids' bedroom doors were closed). I didn't have the slightest idea what she did exactly to keep it so lovely.

It was an idyllic childhood. It also set me up for a crash-and-burn course in housekeeping. In college my roommate and I cleaned up our place when we ran out of clothes. After college I bought a very small house, which I kept clean. I worked hard at keeping it clean. It belonged to me.

When Mark and I married, he had lived on his own for eleven years. He was and is an excellent cook. His clothes have always been well cared for. His checkbook always balances, and his car is immaculate.

At the time of our marriage, I made a mean Kraft Macaroni and Cheese. My clothes were laundered when I ran out of things to wear. My checkbook had not been balanced since I opened the account. My car had room for the driver and a passenger. The back seat was a creative filing cabinet of sorts.

During the early years of our marriage, housekeeping was a breeze. We both worked full time, so we shared the housekeeping jobs equally. We worked together and made it fun. Except for ironing. We both hated ironing.

I'll never forget the time I got off work early and raced home to surprise Mark. Knowing I had four hours before he arrived, I grabbed all the ironing and spent three hours ironing each and every piece.

Mark arrived home to find all my work hanging from the curtain rods. He looked it over, thanked me, and then said these fateful words: "Honey, if you are going to iron my shirts, I don't like a crease on the sleeve."

I gathered my raging emotions and forced them into order. My voice took on a falsely sweet tone. "Fine, dearest. I iron creases into sleeves. If you don't like creases in your shirt sleeves, you may iron your own."

For years Mark did his own shirts. Rather quickly he also saw how much easier it is to go ahead and crease the sleeve like everyone else in the civilized world. It did not soften the heart of his bride. I let him keep ironing those shirts for years, just in case the lesson didn't take.

Several years later I heard a young man ask Mark for advice on his upcoming marriage. Mark said the normal things: Put God first, love her as Christ loves the church, make time to date her even after you're married, etc. Then he threw in a zinger. "And never, under any circumstances, criticize the way she irons!"

Back to the committee. By the time Rachael was born, I had two children in diapers who weren't yet walking, no income, a house that looked like a disaster zone, and out-of-control emotions. I desperately needed help. At the heart of it, I needed to understand that this new hat I wore, the one marked "homemaker," was another sacred crown.

One of my tutors came in the form of a book. It was Christmas Day, and my sister Joanne had given Mom a special little book written by Sue Bender called *Plain and Simple*. The book is Bender's journey to the Amish. She is given the unique opportunity to live with an Amish family and absorb their culture up close.

Christmas afternoon I curled up in Mom's reading chair. A cup of tea rested on the table beside me; the babies slept in the other room. It was that wonderful time of day when the festivities have taken their toll and everything becomes quiet and still. I picked up Mom's new book and began to read.

Many books provide enjoyment. This book nourished deep places inside me. The author writes of the Amish, "No distinction was made between the sacred and the everyday....their life was all one piece. It was all sacred and all ordinary."

Those words stirred something deep inside me. *No distinction. All sacred. All ordinary.* I thought of how many times I had been asked when I would return to work. The tone always implied, "When will your work be sacred again? When will you be a contributing member of society?" The error of that thinking came in a flash. I had spent precious time feeling guilty. But instead of feeling guilty for not having served my Lord in the running of my home, I was feeling guilty for being at home. Guilty and defensive.

Scripture had already told me I was a child of God—born of God. Anything I do is sacred. It may look ordinary from the outside; it may even look mundane and worthless. The spiritual significance of it is far different. The God-breathed reality is that anything His children do is sacred work—set aside for Him.

This caused a revolution in me. I began to see toilet cleaning as a sacred trust. Yes, go ahead and smile. It does look ridiculous on paper, but Scripture had instructed me that *whatever* I did, I was to do it for God. Toilet cleaning represents the lowest form of labor I do. If it was important to Jesus, it would jolly well become important to me.

I decided that I would run my home as unto the Lord. My tasks were holy; I would enter them wholly.

My first task was to make life as easy as possible for the members of my family. Mark's mother is a whiz with babies' schedules. Each time she visited, she got my babies on wonderful schedules: up at 7:00, fed, bathed, morning nap at 10:00, lunch at 12:00, naps at 2:00, dinner at 5:30, and bed at 7:00. She taught me the importance of running things on a schedule. How she got the babies to comply remains a mystery.

Mark's father, Luke, stepped in to help in a gentle teasing way. Our first Christmas together he went out and bought his new daughter-in-law a Christmas present, refusing to show anyone what it was. It was special—from him to me.

He presented it with great fanfare. Everyone stopped what they were doing to see what Papa Luke had given Carol. I nervously unwrapped the parcel. It was an illustrated cookbook. You know, with pictures. Luke grinned and said, "I thought if you knew what it was supposed to look like…well, you know!" Everyone laughed, and I gave Papa Luke a kiss and a thank-you. To this day it is my favorite cookbook. The illustrations really do help! The next Christmas Papa Luke joined that heavenly cloud of witnesses, cheering on our homemaking efforts from an eternal perspective.

With the help of a cookbook, Pat stepped in to teach me how to make menus and save money at the grocery store. Ernestine taught me about celebrations. Wendy instructed in the garden. Mom taught an eager daughter how to keep a clean house. She taught gently and with amazing tact.

Each of these people helped me organize my new work place. The home had replaced the classroom, and I began to realize that if I wanted to succeed, I had to work at it with the same dedication and drive I had applied to my teaching job. As a child I had memorized Colossians 3:23-24: "Whatever you do, work at it with all your heart, as working for the Lord, not for men, since you know that you will receive an inheritance from the Lord as a reward. It is the Lord Christ you are serving." This section of the Bible put it all in perspective.

I began to search for the holy in the daily grind. How could I honor the Lord through my daily tasks?

I read in 1 Corinthians 14:33 about how the church should conduct its services. The verse called for order, saying, "For God is not a God of disorder but of peace." I was fascinated with the contrast. Disorder as opposed to peace. The fruit of the Spirit is peace. I wanted a peaceful home. Apparently I needed to bring that home into order—in each room, in all of my housekeeping jobs, in our schedules. Order in our home would honor God.

As an adult I have learned that once the truth of Scripture has been revealed to a person, it's best to move on that truth quickly. I took what I had learned from the committee and married it to the concept that whatever work I chose to do was to be done as if for the Lord. It didn't take long to get the general hang of it.

Within a few months dinner was a common occurrence. Breakfasts for adults were implemented. Laundry found a place in the schedule, as did reading. Interesting pair, laundry and reading, isn't it? Everything I studied told me it was important to nourish myself as well as the children, or a crash was imminent. The principle is not unlike the instructions they give you on an airplane: "Make sure you secure your own oxygen mask before you put one on your child. You need to remain conscious to help your child." For me reading is a mental health cure. It keeps me conscious. So I took the advice to heart and scheduled down time each day as well as work time.

Eventually the routine became so reasonable that I added an in-home business to the mix. An answering machine found a home on my kitchen desk, and files grew in a cardboard box under the kitchen table.

It all ran reasonably well until March 1988. It was then we learned we were going to be parents. Again. In October. Sometime in October I would be the mother of an infant, a twenty-two-month-old, and a thirty-four-month-old. Two in diapers, three under age three. So much for order.

During this pregnancy I began to study Proverbs 31. The "wife to beat all wives" chapter. I thought the study would encourage and motivate me in the race to achieve supermom status. I have since decided that the supermom myth is an evil story perpetrated by the enemy of women's souls. But at the time I saw in Proverbs a woman who works with eager hands, is a gourmet cook, an early riser, a businesswoman, and is physically fit; she sews, feeds the poor, works late into the night, speaks with wisdom, makes an excellent profit, teaches faithfully, and never eats the bread of idleness.

Couple that study with morning sickness. I think you get the picture. I did not think she was a very necessary part of Scripture, and I did think I was a slug.

Enter the committee. One member asked about my study. She said she didn't think we were supposed to take Proverbs 31 as literally one person. The thought of it being just one woman was depressing to her. She said it was a composite of many women. I began to breathe easier.

The second committee member laughed at my study. She laughed! Out loud! She said I had it all wrong. "This is the picture of a woman's life over the long haul," she comforted. "Sometimes she rose early, no doubt when she had a nursing baby, and sometimes she worked late into the night. For a season she was a businesswoman. For a season she taught. After many seasons she spoke with wisdom."

I began to smile. "Really? You mean I don't have to be all those things tomorrow morning?"

"Really," she said. "You only have to be Megan and Rachael's mommy tomorrow morning."

We paused. Comforted. Reassured.

Then, unable to resist the tease, she went on. "And Mark's wife, and Bill and Nancy's daughter, and Joanne's sister, and Betty's employee, and the children's ministry coordinator, and the chief cook and bottle washer!"

We laughed. Relieved somehow. The impossible made possible by taking tiny steps. The routines of life reinforcing the miraculous. Ordinary jobs becoming sacred, holy occupations.

The following pages are a guide for you to identify areas of clutter and chaos in the daily details of your family life. Use them prayerfully. Resist the urge to skip over them. You purchased this book because something inside you craves more of the Savior. Follow that craving. Rush to meet Him in the small but significant details of your life.

1. List the areas of your life that feel disorganized, cluttered, chaotic.

2. Who can help you organize or learn the tricks of homemaking in these areas?

3. When will you ask them to help you?

4. Lord, here and now I commit to asking the above people for help. More than anything I need your guidance and the guidance of your daughters. Please help me with these significant daily details.

Signed_____

5. What areas of your life feel sacred to you?

6. How can you enhance them? Make them more regular? Share them with others?

7. What areas of your life feel ordinary, mundane, and definitely not sacred?

8. Take some time to study Colossians 3:23-24. Memorize these verses. Ask God to empower you to make this passage a reality in your life.

CHAPTER FIVE

SABBATH

February 1987

Whatever happened to Sunday? Isn't it supposed to be a day of rest? The Jewish rabbis used to say that on the Sabbath the entire world is "resouled." I could use a revitalized soul. But Sundays aren't a day of rest in our family.

Take last Sunday. We arrived at church on time for once, both babies in tow. We decided finally to check out the nursery. We found one woman and what looked like twenty babies between the ages of three days and three years. Our shoulders drooped with defeat. Sighs escaped weary chests.

We walked back to the sanctuary with the two babies in our arms and headed for the back rows where all the other parents of small children hang out. Mark read my mood correctly. He settled Megan on the floor with some toys and then leaned over.

"Honey, if Rachael acts up, I'll take her out. You need to sit through a service. Okay?"

"Ummm..." I nodded, too tired to discuss it.

The worship began. Rachael rested in my arms, a sweet bundle, sound asleep. We began that wonderful praise chorus "Majesty, Worship His Majesty." Within a few lines I felt my spirit soar. This was actually wonderful. To be in the courts of the Lord, a sweet baby at my feet, another joy in my arms, and Mark at my side. The song shifted, and my spirit rose even further. It was wonderful. Heavenly. It was over.

Rachael needed her diaper changed. Mark reached for her and the soft liquidy stuff ran out of her diaper onto my dress. My shoulders drooped, my eyes filled, and my lips quivered.

Poor Mark. He would have done anything to spare me this experience. He didn't even smile. He wrapped me—carefully—in his arms and whispered, "I'm so sorry."

In the Mommy's room I changed Rachael. She actually smiled and cooed while I mopped myself up the best I could and found a rocker. I cracked the curtain and turned on the speaker. I had just settled in when two sweet women arrived to nurse their babies. And talk.

"Hi, Carol. Hey, would you mind turning down that speaker just a bit?" Before I knew it, the entire service had passed in a discussion of babies' sleeping schedules and when to introduce solid food.

We came home tired. Lunch? I remember those beautiful dinners Mom used to make, those afternoons at fancy restaurants with Mom relaxing too. We came home, stuck bottles in the girl's mouths, wolfed down peanut butter and jelly, and went to bed.

What has become of our Sundays? Sunday used to be the crown of the week. It used to cap off and celebrate the week we had just experienced. Now it's an exercise in disappointment.

Lord, don't you miss our time? Don't you see us struggling? Where are You in all of this? Please, send me someone who can take this mess and make it holy again. I want to sit at your feet. HELP!

This journal entry is fairly typical of our Sunday experiences. Oh, it changes. Children cease to wear diapers, but then the morning starts off with tornadoes of activity as we scamper to dress, feed, and keep reasonably clean three small children. By the time the children are all out of diapers, we run children's ministries and are seldom in the church service at all.

During this time I begged God to return to us the holy times of Sundays past. I had loved Sundays. Now I had trouble enduring them. Enter the committee.

Ernestine began to teach on the Sabbath. Genesis 2:2-3 reads, "By the seventh day God had finished the work he had been doing; so on the seventh day he rested from all his work. And God blessed the seventh day and made it holy, because on it he rested from all the work of creating that he had done."

A day of rest. Modeled for us by the Creator Himself prior to the Fall of man. A pattern for eternity. A pattern needed for all of us, for all time. My thoughts gained momentum. What was rest? Real rest?

Webster's says rest is "ease or inactivity after exertion, relief from anything distressing, tiring; absence of motion; refreshment; to become still; quiet, full of peace." Webster's rest and Carol's Sundays had little in common. Actually, nothing in common. I needed a day to recover from Sunday. Here was Scripture telling me that my Sunday should be recovery time. I looked further.

Exodus 31:12-16 says this:

> Then the LORD said to Moses, "Say to the Israelites, 'You must observe
> my Sabbaths. This will be a sign between me and you for the gener-
> ations to come, so you may know that I am the LORD, who makes you
> holy.
>
> "'Observe the Sabbath, because it is holy to you. Anyone who des-
> ecrates it must be put to death; whoever does any work on that day
> must be cut off from his people. For six days, work is to be done, but
> the seventh day is a Sabbath of rest, holy to the LORD. Whoever does
> any work on the Sabbath day must be put to death. The Israelites are
> to observe the Sabbath, celebrating it for the generations to come as a
> lasting covenant.'"

This commandment came with a stiff penalty—death to the person who
desecrates it. I wonder how many of us are working out our own penalties in
diseases that stem from stress, from a lack of rest. What began as concrete pun-
ishments must not be dismissed with the thought that we live in a more
enlightened era. Doctors tell us the importance of rest and relaxation cannot
be exaggerated. Certainly the God of heaven did not make light of it.

I sat up straighter and paid much more attention to the words of Scripture.
I was on to something.

I began to wonder if, just possibly, Sabbath was a Jewish thing. Maybe it
was never meant for Gentiles. Maybe. It was a possibility.

Isaiah 56 put an end to the question. Verses 6 and 7 read: "And foreigners
who bind themselves to the LORD to serve him, to love the name of the LORD,
and to worship him, all who keep the Sabbath without desecrating it and who
hold fast to my covenant—these I will bring to my holy mountain and give
them joy in my house of prayer." Sabbath was created for all of God's children.

I feel compelled to stop here and define the concept of Sabbath. When I
have shared our Sabbath experiences publicly, the audience has become
embroiled in a tense discussion of what the word *Sabbath* means and the historical arguments it represents. We never get to the good stuff. We never
discuss what makes Sabbath holy, or how to practice the presence of God in a
concentrated way on Sabbath. We have just argued and discussed which day
was Sabbath. I would hate for that to happen here.

Mark and I believe that Sabbath is a twenty-four-hour day of rest. It begins
our week. We take that time period from sundown Saturday to sundown

Sunday. Our church worships on Sunday morning and again on Sunday evening. If we belonged to a church that worshiped on Saturday, we would observe Sabbath from Friday evening to Saturday evening. We firmly believe the day of the week is not the issue. The issue is setting aside a day to vacation with God.

Isaiah holds wonderful promises for those who keep the Sabbath—promises that set my imagination on fire. "If you keep your feet from breaking the Sabbath and from doing as you please on my holy day, if you call the Sabbath a delight and the LORD's holy day honorable, and if you honor it by not going your own way and not doing as you please or speaking idle words, then you will find your joy in the LORD, and I will cause you to ride on the heights of the land and to feast on the inheritance of your father Jacob" (Isaiah 58:13-14).

Riding on the heights of the land. Feasting on the inheritance of your father Jacob. What rich images! What a banquet! I wanted to ride those heights. I decided to find out how.

The first thing Mark and I did was to sit down and share our history. He came from a family where Sundays were a day set aside for worship and family. I came from a family with a few notable differences.

My grandmothers were keepers of the Law. To be fair to them, it was a different time. They lived in a different world, and they each loved and followed Jesus to the best of her ability. But I grew up with some early memories of restrictive Sundays.

Grandma Jo used to say, "If you sew on Sunday, you'll take it out with your nose on Monday." Considering my sewing capabilities, she was a prophet. Grandma Wiitala took Grandma Jo's philosophy and added to it. Sundays were for church, big meals, long naps, hymns, radio preachers, and evening service. In a pinch deacons' meetings were allowed. They were all that was allowed. It wasn't fun for a child.

In my immediate family things were looser…but not much. When I was small, stores were not open on Sunday. By the time I was in high school, all the major malls were calling my name. I can still remember hearing our family debate the morality of going to a mall on Sunday. The argument went something like this:

"But, Dad!" (The word *dad* is said in a descending whine.) "We are taking our rest at the mall!"

"Carol, you seem to forget that your leisure is forcing someone else to work on Sunday. Does that seem fair to you?"

Dad learned never to ask his sixteen-year-old daughter about shopping and morality in the same breath. I was certain it was not only fair but, in a great cosmic way, ordained.

Mark and I wanted to find a balance. We remembered Jesus' words in Mark 2:27: "Then he said to them, 'The Sabbath was made for man, not man for the Sabbath. So the Son of Man is Lord even of the Sabbath.'" This verse gave us permission to design days that would be creative and fun, life-giving and restoring. Now all we had to do was find out how.

Ernestine continued her teaching on the Sabbath. She said that Sunday began much earlier than sunrise. She told us her routine: meal preparation on Saturday, clothes ready, house clean. Even though my prayer journal cried out for God to send me help with organizing my time and my home responsibilities, I interpreted her teaching as important only for those in full-time Christian work. I assumed that only pastors needed that kind of Sabbath preparation. If the truth be told, I don't think I relished the extra work. So I let it slide.

Two full years passed by. We struggled. We patted the concept of Sabbath on the head like a pet monkey. Nice little concept. Sweet idea. We did not stop to learn it.

Finally, in 1990 I found a wonderful book called *Making Sunday Special*, which is Karen Mains' story of her and her family's search for order and rest on the Sabbath. As they practice what David Mains calls the "rhythm of the sacred," they find the Lord of the Sabbath.[1] I read this book and knew down to my bones that the Savior was speaking directly to me. I knew this was the answer Mark and I had been searching for. Mark read the book and agreed. We began, piece by piece, to implement Sabbath in our little family, launching an adventure of epic proportions.

First we studied Jewish writers. Rosten said, "to 'make Shabbes' means to be festive, to celebrate." Herman Wouk said, "For me it is a retreat into restorative magic." Those phrases—"festive," "celebration," "restorative magic"—caught my attention. They described what I wanted my family to experience. I wanted them to experience the God who turned water into wine. I wanted them to know the God who instituted holidays and great celebrations. I wanted them to know what it is to be in the very presence of God and never leave the living room.

Wouk continued by saying, "The great difference between the Puritan Sabbath and the even more restrictive Jewish Shabbat is an impalpable but overwhelming one of spirit. Our Sabbath opens with blessing over light and wine. Light and wine are the keys to the day. Our observance has its solemnities, but the main effect is release, peace, gaiety, and lifted spirits."[2]

This was it. Not a Jewish remembrance in a Christian home, but a celebration that mirrors the great feast to come. One with gaiety and lifted spirits. One that celebrates life and light.

Many Christian theologians say that Sabbath is the earthly preparation for the Wedding Feast of the Lamb, that great day to come when Jesus and His Bride are united. I believe this. Wouk writes of Sabbath, "The Sabbath is a bride, and nightfall the wedding hour, so that every Friday at dusk pious Jews read the sparkling love poetry of the Song of Songs."

I was sold. The Brazos would begin to keep the Sabbath.

The keeping of the Sabbath seems to have a rhythm to it. Orthodox Jews look at their week as Sabbath, followed by three days to reflect on what God did on the Sabbath. Then there are three days to anticipate the next Sabbath. My entire being seemed to respond to this rhythm. Mark liked it, I loved it, and the children were too young to cause any trouble over it. We implemented it.

I would love to tell you that all my disappointments were over. Not so. It would take me years to get the hang of it in daily living. We would institute Sabbath, determined to follow it. We would operate in it for several months, and then summer would come, and we would get confused and lose it.

I am writing this book in 1994. Sabbath is pretty much the norm for us now. We all love it. The children adore it and are very unhappy if our schedule gets crazy and we miss it. There are still weeks when we bomb out, when we grab a pizza and look at each other in despair, but more times than not, those twenty-four hours are spent on holy ground. We leave it sadly, having spent uninterrupted time at the feet of the Savior. We anticipate it with great pleasure. Mark feels freedom from guilt on the Sabbath—freedom to look around at the multitude of jobs that need to be done and put his feet up and watch a baseball game. He says that the freedom to relax is one of the most important works of God in his life on Sabbath.

And now we have friends who ask to come have Sabbath with us. The richness of the day of rest, the joyfulness of the celebrations, the quiet time spent at His throne are treasures worthy of a king. And they are ours. Every week.

That is our story. Here is how it happens. The starting point is preparation. Webster's defines *preparing* as "making ready." Remember the parable of the ten virgins? Five made ready their lamps. Five were foolish and did not prepare sufficiently to meet their bridegroom. They grew weary and fell asleep. When the cry went out that the bridegroom was coming, they all awoke and trimmed their lamps. Five had the oil necessary. Five did not. The foolish virgins begged the wise ones to share the oil. The wise ones refused and sent the foolish virgins to buy their own oil. When the foolish ones returned, the bridegroom had already come and gone into the feast. The door was shut to them. They couldn't go into the feast.

Make no mistake. This story is of great importance when it comes to instituting Sabbath in your own home. When we take Sunday casually and adopt a hit-or-miss attitude, we are usually out buying oil when the bridegroom comes. We never know the fullness of His presence the way those who have prepared for it do.

Preparing for Sabbath begins on Thursday at our house. I check the menu, make sure my housework is going according to schedule, and pray about the scripture we have decided to concentrate on. On Friday I do heavy housecleaning. My laundry is finished, and with a little luck so is the ironing! I continue to pray about the scripture we will study and how to teach the children this scriptural lesson. On Saturday I do a quick clean-up, vacuum, and dust. Then I head to the kitchen and prepare a dessert, salad, vegetable dish, and main meal. Our big dinner is eaten Saturday evening; Sunday afternoon is leftovers or a small lunch prepared on Saturday. Sunday evening in our house is popcorn or nachos, apples, and dessert. It's light but yummy. Usually we have eaten so well for the last twenty-four hours that Sunday evening is totally casual.

Preparing my home physically may seem ridiculous to some. Yet I am following centuries of tradition when I do this—centuries of women preparing. That preparation often means saying no to long phone conversations on Friday. But it's worth it.

Preparing my home as if God would physically walk through the front door is a discipline. It is also a gift I give myself. Each week around three o'clock on Saturday afternoon, I walk through my lovely little house. Children are napping, and usually so is Mark. Dinner is ready to go into the oven. Dessert waits on the stove. Each room is gleaming and in order. My study Bible waits by my favorite chair along with my prayer journal. The house takes on a special glow.

During the week the hours from three to seven o'clock are exhausting. They are packed with work and people and chaos. On Saturday, for those few short hours, all of the work, all of the chaos is set aside. Everything in me relaxes. A smile steals across my face and stays there. Frequently I take up my cross-stitch for the first time all week and settle down to create one line of beauty.

Around six o'clock the answering machine goes on. It's amazing. The more people hear of our Sabbaths, the less the phone rings. I've had acquaintances say, "I was going to call on Sunday, but I've heard that you keep a Sabbath of some sort, so I waited till today to call." I'm always amazed at people and their individual thoughtfulness. Imagine having people honor something they do not understand. We do listen to the phone messages just in case someone really needs us. But a vacation from the phone is as important to me as a day away from the office is for Mark.

Finally it's time. The family gathers around the dining room table. I use my prettiest dishes; the table is lovely. There are candles waiting to be lit. Often we play recorded music.

The evening meal is considered the feminine aspect of Sabbath. In a Jewish home Sabbath is welcomed with the words, "May Israel rest in her." It is a time of food and fellowship. The mother lights the candles—the first to observe the Sabbath, the second to remember the Sabbath. Then she thanks God for the Sabbath and asks His blessing on her family—blessings of health, peace, and honor.

At our table I light the candles and then ask the blessing. While we eat, each child is asked to share the experiences she/he has had with Jesus the previous week. Although my children are five, six, and seven, their answers are at times absolutely profound. And not just because I'm their mother. Sometimes their answers make no sense at all. But we never question or correct; we simply let them tell their stories and honor them with complete attention. Then Mark and I share the spiritual highlights of our week. The company is also invited to share. They're never pressured, just invited.

We have had wonderful moments around the table with guests. I believe children soften the heart. Their honest and sometimes humorous sharing breaks down walls in the rest of us and lets us enter the kingdom of God as children also. We are allowed mistakes and humor because they are allowed mistakes and humor. It is frequently true that a child leads us, at least at our house.

After dinner we quickly load the dishwasher and head toward the living room. *We* load the dishwasher. Sabbath is rest for everyone, and we all participate in clean-up.

Two years ago the Lord blessed us with a house that has a family room. The living room has become something of an adults' room. It is always clean, and the children are not allowed to play in it. Sabbath lessons are taught there because it's a special place for the children. After the children's lesson is over, I serve dessert. Then the kids are hustled off to bed, and the adults begin to discuss the scriptural passage we've been meditating on since Thursday.

Later, we head to bed with the words of the Savior dancing in our heads. We always seem to come away with so much more than we entered the discussion with. Often we are in awe and find sleep difficult. Sometimes we get up, make hot tea, and talk over other issues—areas that have been plaguing our marriage or our family. Hearts that are quiet and open can often see the solution, and many times family business is done in those late-night sessions.

Sunday morning I pop frozen breakfast rolls into the oven and serve fresh fruit and orange juice. Amazing what preparation does. We seldom leave with the sounds of fighting ringing in our ears. We head into the church service with hearts full of anticipation. We have been at His feet and He has met us. What does He have planned for this morning? It's always something unique and perfect for the day.

This year we've had a friend come for Sabbath with some regularity. She is single; her children are grown. This wonderful treasure sings in the Portland Opera chorus and plays the flute. The first time she joined us, the evening went pretty much the way I've described. She was enjoying it. While the children ate their dessert, she pulled out her flute and sat me at the piano. Now, my piano skills are elementary. We put some worship choruses in front of me and together we played. The children were mesmerized. Clad in jammies, they lay on the floor and sang the songs. Then Marky (no, not Mark—she's Marky) took the flute and taught each one how to blow into it. Their eyes grew big. No one horsed around. Each took the flute as if it were solid gold. They eyed Marky as if she were a queen. When they finished, they scuttled off to bed in silent awe.

Marky, Mark, and I laughed together. I served dessert, and the conversation became nostalgic. We had a wonderful time, but we never got around to the passage of Scripture we had planned to discuss.

Marky spent the night and accompanied us to church the next morning. A guest speaker took the pulpit and asked us to turn to Luke 24:13. Mark jabbed my arm. I glanced at the scripture and grinned. I nudged Marky.

"What?" she whispered.

"Look at the scripture," I said.

"Okay. What about it?"

"It's the one we were supposed to discuss last night!"

"Really! It really is," she said, eyes sparkling. "Do you really think...?"

"I really know," I said, smiling. Holy ground. God intervening to play catch-up for us. His timing proved perfect once again.

To me it's essential that Sabbath never become a time of rules and restrictions. We view work on the Sabbath as school for Mark, anything around the house or herb business for Carol, anything that is a struggle for the children. Some, including my dear Grandma Jo, might not appreciate my cross-stitching on the Sabbath. Cross-stitching is a luxury to me. A joy. If it feeds that part of us that creates, that celebrates beauty, it is allowed at our house.

Sabbath is a time of wonder and healing. We had missed Sabbath for six weeks in a row last year. Just as we started back into the groove, we received a call from Mark's brother-in-law. He was coming to Portland for a conference and wanted to come over and spend Saturday night with us before he had to fly back early Sunday morning. Could he stay with us?

I had my heart set on Sabbath. Mark explained it to Len and asked if he would mind participating in it. Len graciously agreed. He arrived on Saturday afternoon, and the children smothered him. They adore him, and he is very good with them. Len and Jan have a son the same age as Rachael.

Mark and Len are two men of God who had never really connected. Both love the Lord. Both are dedicated to His service. Both love Len's wife, Jan. They are nice to each other, kind and considerate, but their relationship hadn't gone deeper than that.

After a full afternoon of kids and nosy questions from me, we finally sat down to dinner. The children shared. Mark shared. I shared. Then Len shared, and I began to sense another presence at the table. I began to sense the presence of my Lord opening doors.

The children finished and clamored to begin the story. The two men continued to share their hearts. The discussion was absolutely captivating. I shushed the kids and sent them off. We sat at the table until the discussion was finished.

When it was done, Mark had shared his thoughts, and Len had shared his vulnerabilities. A fragile sense of wonder enveloped me, almost as if I had witnessed a birth. My husband was viewing his brother-in-law with new respect and love. Len was relaxed in a way I had never known him. The man Jan loves was suddenly clearly visible. Love was growing right there in my dining room.

Finally we moved to the living room and taught the children. Then we discussed the scriptural passage, and the man Jan loves revealed himself again. A vulnerable giant. A jewel. And fragile bonds were woven that night, right there in my living room. The Son who had prayed in John 17:23, "May they be brought to complete unity to let the world know that you sent me and have loved them even as you have loved me," had sent His spirit to my living room to bring unity. To bring a new respect. To birth genuine love.

A beginning. And because we are family, there are years for the seedling to grow to maturity.

Sabbath teaching takes on a life of its own. You may plan all you want, but the truth is that the Spirit of God will come and teach the real lessons. Mark and I often look at each other in wonder as the Lord takes our small lessons and explodes them into life-changing experiences.

This last February is a good example. We decided it was time to teach the children all about love. How their mommy and daddy fell in love. What their home was founded on. Oh, we got all holy and worked out this super little lesson and thought we knew it all. (Who's the child here?)

The first night we told them about our courtship and marriage. At the dinner table Mark always blesses each of us, which involves praying a special blessing into our lives. That week Mark had watched me struggle with a friend's opinions about my life. They felt all wrong to me, but I did not want to harm our friendship. I had prayed about them and still felt she was off base. Because of that, Mark prayed I would learn to look only to Jesus for the final answers, that I would not let people who are not invested in my life sway me.

After dinner we showed the children the tape of our wedding. The little girls were in "little girl heaven." They just loved it. Noah...well, Noah played with his Legos. At the end of the ceremony, our principal and his wife came forward to give us a blessing. They told us their prayers for us. Mary Lee prayed that I would always look to Jesus for my answers, that I wouldn't let anyone else sway me.

My eyes filled with tears. Mark squeezed my hand. Twice in one night the same message. Megan, ever the observer, said, "Mom, what's wrong now?"

Mark replied for me, "Megan, do you remember what Daddy prayed for Mommy tonight at dinner? I prayed that she would learn to look first and foremost to Jesus to tell her if her life is acceptable. Mommy sometimes lets too many people try to change her. She needs to learn to listen to Jesus as her first and largest priority. On the tape just now a woman prayed the same prayer for Mommy. Mommy has had people praying that prayer for her for a long time!"

Megan's eyes got big. "But Dad. You guys got married a LONG time ago!"

Poor Megan. She never did understand why her father and I both started to laugh. But she did understand that Jesus really knew and understood her mama.

God was not done modifying our lesson plans. The next week Mark was going to teach the children the foundations of our marriage and family. He told the children how he had asked Mommy to marry him by sending her a telegram. Then he told them Mommy and Jesus had spent much time talking about our marriage. He told them Mommy's greatest prayer was that Jesus would give Mommy and Daddy "one heart" in all their decisions.

Finally he got out the Lincoln Logs. He took four cornerstones (blocks) and played with them until the children had memorized their names: loving, adoring, cherishing, one heart—the words of his marriage proposal and the cornerstone of our life together. And then we built a house. A Lincoln Log house. There, for all of us to see, were our foundations—our cornerstones. When we had finished, Mark quieted everyone.

"Kids, what do you think would happen if we stopped cherishing each other?" he asked. And before the kids could answer, he pulled the cherishing cornerstone out from under the house.

We all watched as the house slid into a fragile state at one corner.

"Not very good, is it?" he asked.

Three somber little heads shook back and forth.

"But you could still live there, right?"

"Right, Dad," the kids chorused.

"What do you think would happen if we also stopped adoring each other?" Mark continued. And once again, before we could reply, he pulled the adoring cornerstone out from under the house. This time the house completely fell apart. Splat.

The kids were really quiet. "It doesn't take much to destroy a home, does it?" he asked. Then he went on to talk about the ways he had seen us failing to cherish and adore and love. He also talked about the ways he *had* seen us cherish, adore, and love. He asked us to try to have one heart, and then we stopped and asked Jesus to give us one heart.

The whole lesson took less than fifteen minutes but remains forever fixed in my heart. You see, Mark and I did not think the house would fall on a failure to adore. We knew it would be hard to live in a house with two cornerstones missing, but we thought the house would not fall until love was removed. The Savior had come to teach us, not just the kids. Cherishing and adoring are priorities with Him in our lives. You may determine other foundations for your home, but these are uniquely ours. And the Savior Himself had come to teach us.

Not all Sabbaths are spent in our home. We've camped on Sabbaths, had Sabbath dinner at the drive-in, had Sabbath at the beach. We believe it's the spirit of the Sabbath that's important, not a list of rules and regulations. And no matter where we are or what the agenda is, the Lord of the Sabbath is present in a special way. Weaving His lessons. Whispering His love. Wooing His bride.

Karen Mains writes, "Sunday is a holy festival that foreshadows the one great celebration supper of the wedding feast of the bride and the Lamb." When Mark and I approach Sundays with that in mind, it's impossible not to be aware of its significance—its holiness and honored place in God's creation. We will someday celebrate the wedding feast of the Lord Jesus Christ and His bride. I want my family to be familiar with that concept. So we have rehearsals of heaven. The temporal mirroring the eternal. Every week. At our house.

Today is Friday. I will shortly leave this computer screen to shop for Sabbath. I can't tell you our lesson this week. On Wednesday morning the children asked if they could teach the Sabbath lesson. They wanted to teach on what it means to be a spiritual man and how a spiritual man builds his house. I wish you could join us tomorrow night. I can guarantee you, I will be in the presence of the King. Ushered into the realm of His kingdom by children. Made to understand profound truth by the teaching of babes. Resouled.

The following pages outline a simple Sabbath for you and your family, designed for minimum fuss and maximum time at the feet of Jesus.

• Sabbath is a gift we give ourselves. Begin by listing the jobs around the house that need to be done if Jesus were to physically walk into your home this weekend.

• Assign each job the following: how long it will take, who will do it, when it needs to be done, and who will applaud the work.

• Menus: Plan a special meal for Sabbath evening, then plan Sunday breakfast, leftovers for lunch, and casual food for the evening. Choose food that will not require a lot of work during the twenty-four-hour break.

SABBATH: THURSDAY

1. Assess housework. Is it on schedule? Plan menu and clothes for the children.

2. Begin to meditate on a chosen scripture. How will you teach it to your children? What truth do you want them to know? For example, when we chose Matthew 14:13-21, we talked about the fact that some children do not have enough food. So we decided to sponsor a child through World Vision and made a bank for all our spare change.

FRIDAY

1. Do final housecleaning, go grocery shopping, remind the family that Sabbath is coming.

2. Finalize how you plan to teach the children the chosen scripture.

SATURDAY

1. Do a quick vacuum and then to the kitchen. Prepare all the food. By three o'clock try to sit down and relax.

2. For dinner have at least two candles ready to be lit. As the mom, light the candles and thank God for this time of rest, or have another adult female do so. Ask God for the blessings of health, peace, and honor. Then serve dinner. During dinner have Dad tell each member of the family how he or she has blessed him this week. If you are a single mom, bless each of your children and then repeat these words, "The Lord Himself is my husband. He is present here tonight. He is pleased with me." Ask each person to share how Jesus was present in his or her life this week.

3. After dinner teach the children the lesson, serve dessert, and tuck the kids in bed. If your children are older, encourage them to stay and listen to the adult discussion. Whether you are married or single, the longer you do Sabbath, the greater the joy of having guests on this holy night. Invite another single mom to come and share the evening. It will lighten both of your loads and encourage you. Remember widows and share this night with them. Look to the larger church and community family to fill vacant places at the table.

4. When the adults have finished, invite everyone, regardless of gender, to head to the kitchen to clean it up. Then serve coffee and tea, and enjoy late night talks.

5. Before you go to bed, check the kids' clothes, making sure that everyone has what he or she needs. Remind yourself of the breakfast menu.

SUNDAY

I like to be up an hour and a half before we leave for church to set out breakfast and supervise, supervise, supervise!

Sunday afternoon is a time of rest. Books are pulled out, games are played, naps are a treat for Mom, and the kids are excused from theirs if they keep quiet. The kitchen is open all day with leftovers and snacks on the counter.

Sunday evening is a quiet time of bidding the Sabbath farewell. People are reflective. The children go to bed, the kitchen is cleaned, and we smile, satisfied. Usually around half past eight Mark and I check our schedules for the coming week and clear things with each other.

If you would like to begin with small, easy steps and progress to having a Sabbath as I just outlined, you could follow this plan:

WEEK ONE

First things first! Concentrate only on the spiritual discipline of having Sabbath. Don't let those words frighten you; the steps are simple.

Listen carefully to the lessons learned in your church Sunday. Take home one idea you feel is worth thinking about. Spend Sunday through Wednesday studying and praying about that one idea. This is the Jewish custom of reflecting on what God has done on the previous Sabbath.

On Thursday begin to read and meditate on one particular passage, such as Matthew 14:13-21. Plan to teach the story to your children on Saturday night. Does the issue of world hunger grab you? Your children could make a list of the things they can contribute to God's family, including the talents they have.

Meditate on this scripture through Saturday night. On Sunday listen carefully at church and begin the process all over again.

WEEK TWO

Add to the discipline of the previous week, meal preparation.

By Wednesday plan a menu for dinner Saturday night that is easy to prepare and enjoyed by the majority of the family. Then plan Sunday's meals, making them a study in "how to keep Mom out of the kitchen!" A day of rest is for everyone. Have fun with it!

Thursday through Saturday meditate on Luke 10:25-37. What lessons does God have to teach you through the story? I had the children think of three things they could do to bless our neighbors that week.

Saturday night put aside as much of the outside world as possible, and open up your hearts for a special encounter with the Savior. Keep the meal conversation upbeat. Tease and laugh and have fun. Then teach the story, serve dessert, and get the kids to bed. Afterwards you and your beloved enjoy the peace and quiet!

Sunday morning go to church expecting to meet your Savior in new ways. Find one part of the sermon or lesson that is worth thinking about for the next three days. Share it with your husband. Find out what part he liked best. Talk to the kids about what you saw and learned.

Sunday afternoon should be a time of rest. Mark and I nap. The kids do not! They are at an age where they can entertain themselves for an hour. Take a walk as a family. Make caramel apples. Do a jigsaw puzzle. The idea is to relax and interact.

WEEK THREE

This week begin to take stock of what is not running smoothly on Sabbath. Usually it is something logistical. For me, it always seems to involve laundry.

On Monday figure out what jobs around the house need to be accomplished to give you a peaceful Sabbath, and assign those jobs. Everyone can and should help, infants excluded, husbands and kids included! Plan when those jobs should be done.

By Wednesday begin meditating on this week's scripture. Luke 8:22-25 is a good one to teach your children. Have they ever been in a storm? Have you ever felt that your life was in danger of being swamped? It is a good time to discuss fear and the faithfulness of God.

On Friday check on those household chores. Who's responsible for that stack of ironing? Plan the clothes everyone will need for Sunday and get them clean and ready.

On Saturday set aside the outside world and prepare to meet Jesus in a new way. Have dinner. Some are lovely, some are not. Don't worry; Jesus was used to barbecuing on the beach.

On Sunday learn something new and commit to rethinking it for the next three days. Spend a quiet afternoon. Reinvent the word "play."

WEEK FOUR

This week add the practice of blessing.

Sunday through Wednesday meditate on the lesson of Sunday. Assign household work, plan the menu for the weekend.

On Thursday begin meditating on Luke 6:46-49. Plan how to teach the children the lessons of careful construction. Use Lincoln Logs or Legos or any construction toy. Think about the construction you've done in your life. What areas need a firmer foundation? Begin to ask the Lord to give strength to those areas.

On Friday check out the work detail. Crack the whip! Find someone else to do the ironing!

On Saturday light candles as you say the blessing over the meal. Thank God for the blessing of light. Have your husband join you in praising each child for good things you have seen in their lives this week. Give them hugs as you tell them. And don't worry; the food will keep.

Teach the story, serve dessert, and get those angels to bed. Tell your husband how he blesses you. Recall your dating days and snuggle up to some warm memories.

On Sunday meditate on the new lessons of God, and begin the process all over again! Four weeks of Sabbath and you'll be a pro.

CHAPTER SIX

NEW DECOR

February 1988

I have spent the last two Saturdays helping women decorate their homes. We've looked through volumes of magazines, books, and sales brochures. We've discussed the need for each room, the people living in it, the best colors, the need for order. Today we spent time picking out pictures that would blend with new wallpapers, trinkets that would bring out the hue in a flower or the color of a pillow sham. I am thoroughly exhausted, body and soul.

I am also completely aware of the importance of beauty in our surroundings. I understand the effect beauty has on the psyche. If a home is devoid of beauty, it leaves me feeling flat, like a deflated balloon. A cluttered home makes me feel tired and deprived of all energy.

And yes, I do use it in manipulative ways. If the kitchen isn't a cheerful place to go...let's eat out! If the bedroom isn't prepared for lovers...I've got a headache. I do understand the need these women feel to pull their homes together.

But homemaking is not just a matter of decor. You do not have to have money to make a home delightful to the spirit. What you need is spirit. You need the Spirit of God.

This, Lord, is what I want. I want my home to reflect you. I am no longer interested in just pretty pictures done in compatible colors. I could care less about collecting the latest rage. I really want the walls of my home to reflect the work of you in my life, in our lives. I want to look up and be reminded of my eternal Bridegroom while I create a meal. I want your presence to be the direct and indirect lighting in every room.

I am incapable of achieving what I want. I can't even put a decent picture to my words. God, all I know is that I want you. I want you in this area of my life as well as the others. Would you come in and decorate my walls? Put new paint on surfaces that have seen only the paint of shallowness. Use deep, true colors. Leave no room untouched. Leave no clutter unorganized. Please, Jesus. Please come and make me a home.

Another cry. Another need. And again, God sends me a committee. No, I did not receive ten thousand dollars in free decorating from the hottest firm in Portland. What I did receive were "pictures" of what I wanted to have in a Christ-centered home and what I wanted to avoid.

The first picture came in the form of a weekend away. We stayed at a beautiful home set on ten or twelve acres. Every room was a study in perfection. The best books lined the living room shelves. The best music played softly all day long. The finest gourmet food left the kitchen to be served in a dining room that was set to perfection. The bedrooms were a lover's paradise. The gardens rivaled those pictured in coffee table books. It was a study in the art of decor.

Two days into the visit I experienced a strange sadness. Aside from the carefully planned beauty of the home, nothing fed my soul. Jesus was not invited, nor was He welcome.

I searched for Him in the garden. I found His creative handiwork, but I didn't find Him. I searched for Him in the kitchen, remembering how He loved to give men food. Not there. Under the stars I found His autograph, but like any homesick love, the postcard was not enough. Eventually I found His presence, but He was only there at my invitation. The owner of the home preferred He be elsewhere.

Conversation at this home was stimulating. Subjects were discussed with tolerance, kindness, and thought. Everything was given the intellectual gift of contemplation and consideration. Every subject, that is, but Him. He was required to stand on the other side of the gate. If He insisted on accompanying me, it was only as a mental patient from the previous century—a person present but not recognized. Hidden in shame; kept silent and out of sight. Far from conscious awareness.

Once my senses had their fill of the beauty, I felt bereft. Political correctness and intellectual conformity lived at this house. Clothed in words and thoughts of the highest and loveliest nature, they littered the hallways and subtly controlled the environment. It left me cold.

While the right words and phrases were voiced with regularity, there was no evidence of the deeper person with struggles and triumphs of his or her own. No understanding of the spirit. Everything was soulish—to feed the senses and intellect. And I began to see clearly the imbalance.

70

The second picture I received was a home that belongs to our dear friends, John and Wendy. It's very similar to the first home, large in size and set on acres of beautiful land. The interior, a reflection of the artistic spirits that inhabit the house. The gardens, suited for a spread in *House Beautiful.* The books are the same quality that line the shelves of the first home, and the food comes in the same amazing varieties.

The difference is not that a cross or Bible verse hangs in a prominent position. The difference is that each room has stories of Jesus and His work in their lives. Books, pictures, rugs, even dishes, tell of His care.

This spring Wendy was given a phenomenal gift. This wonderful mother and wife went to Europe for three weeks to study art. Wendy the artist, sent off to Florence by her husband and her father to live in a centuries old convent and study art. Two men working together to bring out the best of who Wendy is.

John stayed home to watch the kids, run the home, manage the farm, and work. He did a masterful job. Wendy returned to an immaculate house. Everything was up and running. It was as if an efficiency expert had taken over the house and things were in tip-top shape.

Within an hour Wendy's suitcases were open on the living-room floor. Stacks of clothes, presents, books, and pictures cluttered the room. Wendy and the children and John sat in the center of this mess as she told stories of why Jesus had sent her to Florence. From her suitcase she pulled items bought in Rome or Florence or Milan to illustrate the stories. They were tiny memorials to the work of the Spirit of God in the life of this child.

After she finished, she surveyed the room and began to feel badly about the mess. John's perfect house was again a disaster area, flooded with the stories and props that are quintessential Wendy. It was then John paid her the compliment of a lifetime.

"Wendy, I've missed this so much," he whispered.

"This? This mess?" she asked, unbelieving.

"This chaos, this joy, this magic you bring into our lives," he said.

Joyful chaos. Magic. Stories of Jesus. I want what John put a name to. I want the chaos, the joy, the magic that comes from sitting for hours at the feet of the Savior and having that time reflected in the life of my family. In our home.

I confess. My pillows do match the couch. There is an overall color scheme to my house. Candles are chosen for their shapes and colors. But other things have crept into our house as well, things that give honor to the work of God in each of our lives.

It began with Scripture. Deuteronomy 6:6, 12 tells us: "These commandments that I give you today are to be upon your hearts. Impress them on your children. Talk about them when you sit at home and when you walk along the road, when you lie down and when you get up. Tie them as symbols on your hands and bind them to your foreheads. Write them on the doorframes of your houses and on your gates.... Be careful that you do not forget the LORD, who brought you out of Egypt, out of the land of slavery."

The nation of Israel was to record His commandments, His workings in their lives. They were never to forget that Jehovah had brought them out of Egypt. Out of slavery.

I am thirty-six years old. I've had plenty of time to know Egypt. I have lived in the land of slavery. I've sold my soul to several different slave masters. And I have watched my Lord patiently come, lovingly see, and when requested, purchase my freedom. I know Him as Savior.

This knowledge bears a tremendous responsibility: to mark well the path I've traveled. To build remembrances on my walls, on the gates of my house. To teach my children the faithfulness of God in their mother's life, in their father's life, and in the life of our family.

We must write His works on our gateposts. We must talk about the words of God, the workings of God, the love of God—when we rise up, while we work, and when we rest. We must teach them diligently to our children. For this we are responsible.

Joshua 4:21-24 tells us another story. Joshua has just instructed the Israelites to build an altar of stones. This record follows: "He said to the Israelites, 'In the future when your descendants ask their fathers, "What do these stones mean?" tell them, "Israel crossed the Jordan on dry ground." For the LORD your God dried up the Jordan before you until you had crossed over. The LORD your God did to the Jordan just what he had done to the Red Sea when he dried it up before us until we had crossed over. He did this so that all the peoples of the earth might know the hand of the LORD is powerful and so that you might always fear the LORD your God.'"

This is one of many altars—memorials to the workings of God—in the Scriptures. They are powerful reminders of His mercy, His provision. Our homes need to have memorials in them too—physical representations that keep us from ever forgetting His care for us or His power in our lives.

After asking God for help in this area for a while, I was substituting at the local junior high one day. Hanging from ribbons over the teacher's desk were three antique keys. They hung at varying lengths, but each was low enough for me to reach and to swing back and forth.

The students noted my fascination with the keys and asked me about them. It seems the keys were a mystery. No one knew why they were there or why occasionally the teacher added one. There hadn't been any keys at the outset of the year. What was the deal?

I loved those keys. By second period I had solved the mystery, but like any good substitute teacher I kept my mouth shut. The teacher was putting up a key at the beginning of each new term. By my calculations one should have gone up just that week. And indeed, the following week as I walked past the room, one hung there.

I went home thinking about the fascination and excitement the teacher had generated with those keys. Although I sat at the computer and tried to concentrate on work, ten minutes later the monitor was still blank. My eyes had strayed to a wall that has a three-foot-square cut-out, which enables one to see from the kitchen into the family room. Blank space. An indoor window.

Before anyone knew what had happened, I put up three keys, attached to ribbon, in the cut-out. They hung low so that little hands could swing them. The catch was their meaning. I refused to tell anyone, even Mark. They were my very own mystery.

Over the next two weeks I played with the keys, caressing them and asking the kids to tell me the significance of the keys.

"Well, Megan, what do you think they mean?" I asked.

"I dunno, Mom. Do you think it has anything to do with three blind mice?"

"Nope. I don't think so. Keep working on it," I encouraged.

Finally Sabbath arrived and the jig was up. Having everyone totally involved in the mystery, I let them solve it. I explained that each key represented a very important work of God in Mom's life. Each one had a story and each one was important to Mom. Important to God.

The kids were awestruck. "Can we have keys too?" they begged.

I sighed, playing it for all it was worth. "Well, I don't know. Has God done significant work in your life? What would your key represent?"

Over the next few weeks each child came to me with profound reasons for keys of their own. Now, two-and-a-half years later, many keys hang in the cut-out. Most important, each member of the family knows why.

Here are a few of my favorite key stories.

"Mama, Noah asked Jesus into his heart today," Megan sang out from the back of the van.

"Ummm…really?" I asked, nonplussed.

"Yeah, Mommy. They gave me a book to do it! Wanna see?"

"Later, honey. Daddy and I will talk to you about it later." My plan being to talk to him about it twelve months later.

Now, before you take me for hard-hearted and insensitive, you need to understand that Noah is my baby. My girls entered into eternal life at the ages of four and three. I had problems believing their ability to take such a step, but they had proven me wrong.

Four-year-old Noah was not as formal in his reasoning as the girls had been at that age. Besides, he was so different from the girls. Noah is given to making car noises…vroom…vroom…and chasing the bad guys yelling, "I gonna kill you, I gonna kill you." So today he makes a bargain with the Almighty in exchange for a book? I don't think so.

Two days later I was paying bills. Not a fun thing to do. Noah vroomed at my feet with a fire truck and ambulance.

"Mommy, I don't have to be scared to sleep alone in my bed anymore. Wanna know why?" he asked.

"Sure, Noah," my eyes still glued to the debit column. "Why?"

"Jesus said I didn't have to be scared 'cause He would sleep on the top bunk!"

A flicker of delight began to dance in my heart. "Honey, that's great. Did Jesus say anything else?"

"Nope. Vrooommmmm…vrooommmmm…. How do they get the water to the fire?" he continued, on to other important details in the life of a four-year-old.

That night I tucked my towheaded cherub into bed, got a sleepy kiss, and began to leave the room. Halting, I glanced at the top bunk.

"You up there, Lord?" my spirit whispered.

No answer. My smile returned in jaunty fashion. The delight took up its tune.

After five or six nights of this routine, life returned to the mundane. Noah's experience got lost in ballet lessons and trips to the dentist.

Then came the morning of revelation. I was sitting in my favorite chair, sipping tea and reading a great suspense novel, when in walked Noah.

"Mama, are real lions nice?"

Without bothering to look up, I just sent out the programmed Mama-response. "No, Noah. Real lions eat little boys."

"Really, Mama?"

"Really, Noah."

"But Mama, Jesus comes to my room as a lion and says it's okay cuz He won't hurt me. He makes me safe."

The book dropped to my lap. My son is well taught, but I have never covered the symbolism of the Lion of Judah. Now the Lion of Judah is sleeping on our top bunk!

"Noah, say that to me again, honey."

"Never mind, Mama. It's just Jesus." And off he went to play with his Lincoln Logs while his mother sat in stunned awareness of the reality of Jesus in the small heart of Noah.

KEY NUMBER TWO

Mark married me fully aware of what he was getting into. He had told me story after story of snow camping, hiking, and bike trips of a thousand miles. I had told him story after story of shopping trips and Christmas craft sales. My adventures were at least as daring as his, though in a different arena.

When we wed, Mark did not try to change me. He never asked me to camp. He agreed that Holiday Inn had some pretty nice advantages. He understood the draw of the quaint bed and breakfast inns I preferred.

This is not to say we abandoned the great outdoors. We still skied and sunbathed. Skiing was strictly downhill for me. Mark enjoys cross-country skiing, but I have never understood that. What's the attraction? There are no chair lifts to carry your body up the hills. There are only your own two legs. I don't think God made my legs to go up hills…only down. So, we stick with downhill when I'm along. Fine with Mark, great by me.

Sunbathing was also fine. Mark bodysurfed and I magazine surfed. He whipped his body through the waves, and I whipped my eyes through volumes of fluff. We were both content.

Enter the children. Bed and breakfasts do not take babies. Or children. The family income is cut in half. The tent is beginning to look like an option.

Finally, on our tenth anniversary, the choice was upon us. If I wanted to spend four nights at bed and breakfasts, see a play in Ashland, and generally pretend we were on the childless, romantic trip of a lifetime, then the vacation with the kids would have to be in the tent.

Both of our families are veteran campers. So the equipment was provided. The kids were enthused. The mother was quietly doubtful. Oh well, what's a week in the wild? After all, Mark had promised this first trip would include flush toilets.

So off we scampered. Three kids, two dogs, a tent, and a bag of great books. Off to see the world.

We struggled through rain-soaked sleeping bags. We had a memorable Sabbath under the stars. Then, on the last night, Noah and I took a walk.

Hand in hand we walked through the darkness. Above us the stars danced, forming an amazing canopy that seemed to touch the ground.

Noah squeezed my hand. "Mama, how does the sun go down?"

"I don't know, sweetheart. Ask your dad."

"Mama, I think I know how the sun goes down. I think that God's hand pushes it down."

Noah held out his small arm, fingers tight and straight. He demonstrated a slow pushing effort.

"That's great, Noah. I never knew how the sun goes down. Now I do. Just like this, right?" I put my hand out straight and pushed downward.

"That's right, Mom. You got it!" Surprise filled his excited little voice.

We shared a smile, delight coursing through my veins. Taught the natural world by a four-year-old.

My husband is a scientist. He knows all about astronomy, orbits, formulas, and calculations. When we returned, he stood at the camp stove, boiling water for tea.

"Noah, honey, tell Dad about the sunset. Tell him how the sun goes down," I pleaded.

"Dad, know how the sun goes down?" Noah asked.

Standing behind my son, I motioned for Mark to answer in the negative.

"No, Noah. How does the sun go down?" Mark asked.

"Like this! The hand of God pushes it down!" Again the outstretched arm, fingers tight, pressing downward. His expression was one of accomplishment and pride.

Mark made the right noises, applauded his son's thoughts, and shared a smile with me.

That night, under the stars, Mark and I discussed our summer vacation. We laughed at the dogs' antics, our favorite being the time the pup got her head stuck in the tent flap. We discussed the children's play, grateful they were without a VCR. Watching them invent magnificent adventures had reminded us both that the television can also rob children of their childhood. We discussed the things we wanted to remember, like bringing a cutting board and two bars of soap—one for the boys and one for the girls.

We watched the stars, and when we were certain the children were asleep, we stole a kiss or two...or three. It was then, wrapped in my sweetheart's arms, that I said those long awaited words. "Honey, I've loved this. I wouldn't trade these days for anything. Let's do them again. Let's camp with the kids every year."

Mark smiled, eyes alight. His hug tightened into a squeeze. A pact was formed.

Mark, remembering the tribe of chipmunks we'd befriended, said, "I like this campsite. I think we'll come back here again soon."

He nuzzled my neck, and our smiles broadened as we heard a four-year-old voice emerge from the tent. "I think I'll come back here again too, Dad."

KEY NUMBER THREE

"Carol, you must always remember this. You are never too old to hurt your children."

Now why would Patsi's words come back to me today? She had written me those words shortly after my first baby was born. Her parents had finally decided to divorce after thirty years of marriage. It had not been a happy marriage, so the divorce was not a surprise. They had stayed together "for the children," and now the children were grown.

Or were they? Patsi's letter was full of raw, searing pain. At twenty-five she felt abandoned, unloved. She wondered if she bore any of the blame.

Now, almost eight years later, her words fill my mind as I drive home from the hospital. Mom has had surgery on her eye today. The prognosis is good. The surgeon did amazing things, procedures out of a futuristic novel. On my mama. And she will be fine.

I spent the afternoon with Daddy. Arriving at three o'clock, we hoped Mom would be out of surgery within thirty minutes or so. Dad was as he always is. Strong. Confident of God's work in Mom's life. Confident this is all for our good. Certain of her recovery. Grateful that her sight will be saved.

He reminds me that I do not need to sit with him. Not necessary. Mom will be fine. Don't I have a book proposal due? Shouldn't I be home, working on the computer?

I assure him I am doing this for me, not him. He relaxes. We talk about the details of our lives. The kids' latest antics amuse him for a time. The clock on the wall stretches to four. We check the desk. No news.

By half past four the stories are all told. We begin to search for conversation. I notice that while nothing else in Daddy's tone has changed, his foot is tapping. Dad is not a foot tapper. Not unless Johnny Cash is on stage. And Johnny is definitely not in this waiting room.

We continue to talk, and I continue to watch Dad's foot betraying his outward calm. Betraying an inner love and concern for a woman still in surgery.

One of Dad's colleagues comes by. His mother is in for a knee replacement. They discuss the upcoming American Legion baseball tournament. Dad is in charge. They hope the weather will hold. The man promises to keep my mom in his prayers.

Finally, as the hands of the clock signal five, the surgeon returns. He and Dad huddle alone. By Dad's expression and body language, I am certain Mom is fine. He returns to tell me that the eye had much more scar tissue than anticipated. Then he relays the details of optic nerves and silicone bands. A miracle. For Mama.

While she is in recovery, we jet out for a hamburger. He stops to buy her chocolate. Buys me some too. We return, and the woman at the desk seems bewildered by our request.

"I don't think she's out of recovery," she says. "No. See here? They haven't called yet to tell us her room. I'll let you know as soon as they do."

Dad and I each pull out folders of work and begin to attack our mounds of paper. After ten minutes Dad says, "Honey, isn't that a new person at the desk?"

"Yes, it is. Do you want me to ask?"

"I think so. They don't know you," he trails off. Obviously my father hates to be a nuisance.

I return with Mom's room number and off we go, both of us worried she has returned to a room with no family waiting for her. We round the corner and find that our wonderful, detail-assisting God has sent my sister, Joanne. She has been in Mom's room since six. She was there when Mom returned. We smile at each other. The bases were covered.

Mom is out of it. We visit a bit and then quiet down so not to disturb her. Sitting on the windowsill, I pick up the newest novel. A few pages into it, movement catches my eye. Mom's fingers are stretching out. Before I can form the word, Dad is out of his chair, holding her hand. He caresses her hair and whispers to her. The two hands are tightly entwined.

Joanne and I both turn away. We are witnesses to the intimacy of our parents' marriage. Privileged bystanders viewing a scene of intense devotion. Of lifelong adoration. The purity of their love is too fresh, too stark. I feel I am intruding and keep my back turned. The trees outside the window seem to blur, and it is several moments before anyone establishes eye contact again.

We smile. All is right with the world.

So now I am driving home alone. Home to loving arms that will comfort me and soothe away the stress of the day. Home to three children who will clamor to be heard. But Patsi's words keep ringing in my head. Never too old to hurt your kids, never too old.

Finally the tumblers fall into place. Mom and Dad are fifty-six years old. I have not lived in their home for seventeen years, yet they still provide a foundation of security for me. They still pattern lifelong love. Never too old to teach and reassure your children. These two people remain my best teachers. That tapping foot...those outstretched fingers...they will forever be my teachers.

So at our house we hang keys. Keys to our walk with God. Keys to our walks with each other. Reminders of eternal lessons. One small way in which we work to impress the workings of God on our children.

Decorating fads will come and go. The ways of God are changeless. Color combinations, furniture arrangements, floral displays are temporary. Use them. Enjoy them. Be blessed by them. But in using them, in working with the walls of your home, never forget that a home is founded on the spirit of the people who inhabit the building. If the Spirit of God lives in the folks at your house, make sure that is reflected on the walls and gates of your home. Bring the holy home. Let it be evident in every corner of your dwelling.

The following questions are to get your creative juices flowing. Use anything that works for you, and may it bring you and your family the joy it has brought to ours.

1. What lessons has God taught me this year? My spouse? My children?

2. What lessons do I want to have impressed and pictured in the hearts of my children?

3. What symbols do I like? How could God use them to help me reflect His working in our lives?

4. Why am I doing this? Study Deuteronomy 6:1-12 and Joshua 4.

CHAPTER SEVEN

GARDENS

May 1993

I am not a gardener—and all who know me shout "Amen!" I tend to despise the wiggly, squiggly things that make their home in the earth.

My children, God love them, adore the earth. They take ridiculous joy in bringing me treasures from the soil. You've seen those treasures—the kind that have a slimy film covering their bodies. And always, always Mark is present, forcing me into an adult reaction.

"Honey," his first earth lecture began, "you need to be calm when they bring you things. They are just inquisitive children who want to learn. Don't spaz out on them."

I solemnly agree. Anxious to prove myself. Knowing he is right. Again. Worm phobias do pass from mother to daughter to granddaughter to great-granddaughter. I steel myself, praying furiously for calm.

Then it's off to weed we go. Five of us. Mark and I with gardening equipment. The children armed with a look of mischief.

Gardening at our house is a slow process. Mark loves to make things grow. He knows how it works. I love to see a beautiful garden. I do not know how it works. I tend to work hard to dislodge a particularly difficult weed only to be told, "Honey, that cream-colored ball at the bottom is a bulb. Bulbs become flowers. Put it back."

Exasperated and embarrassed, I continue to pull at the things I hope are weeds. Mark, reading my straight back and firm jaw correctly, postpones further education.

"Mommy, Mommy, come quick!" Excited cries fill the air. Little Noah is dancing with enthusiasm. The girls are bent over, heads together in examination. Removing my gardening gloves, I run to join them. Mark stands nearby, watching in restrained amusement.

"Hold out your hands and close your eyes, Mom!" they command.

Giggles and shrieks fill the air as my hand feels something crawling. Before I can scream and fling the thing back to earth, Mark places a restraining hand on my shoulder and begins his reptile lecture.

"Great, kids!" he exclaims. "This is an earthworm. See the segments...." His voice drones on as he holds me forcibly in place and explains the wonders of this small "snake" to three impressionable children. Three little minds now firmly converted to the glories of the reptile kingdom. Ugh.

Eventually I am released from Biology class and return to the gardening gloves that will remain on my hands. But all is not lost. The children are pleased and proud of their discovery. And I am rather proud of my control.

I did a good job of pretending to be a mature adult. I have a steady heartbeat once again. As I stoop to retrieve a spade, the payoff arrives. Two strong arms wrap themselves around me, and I hear tender words of love and praise. A nuzzle on the neck confirms it. This gardening thing is pretty good after all.

Several years ago we lived in a house I hated. I love old things. Antiques. Family recipes. And most of all, those crazy old structures that have nooks and crannies, porches and magical attics.

Mark loves new things. He adores computers and fax machines. His mind is fascinated by them. He loves new construction. He's delighted by all the ways contractors make life easier. He reads *Architectural Digest* and I read *Country Living.*

Our first house was a Carol's delight. Seventy years old. Wonderful angles and crazy rooms. Old windows and built-in bookcases.

Mark loved that house. He really did. It was fun to sleep under the rafters. Not so fun to wake up to a four-foot ceiling though. Not when you're 6'4" tall. It was fun to have an old oak staircase. But not when you had to take it apart to get a bed upstairs and then reassemble it.

Then there was the electrical system and plumbing. What's to complain about? The bathroom was indoors, after all. But Mark got nervous when we realized that if you used the electrical outlet in the bathroom and the outlet in the girls' bedroom in certain ways, at the same time, it shorted out. Every time. For three years. Nope, an old gem is not the house to own when you're just starting out and dead broke.

So the next house was modern. And while Mark was gracious about our first house, I had trouble keeping my mouth shut about the next one. It was a modern monstrosity, which is why we could afford it. Not a good lot. Not a great design. But the plumbing and electrical systems were only three years old. The whole house was only three years old.

What bothered me most was the "professionally landscaped yard." Yes, that's a Realtor's description. If I had been the "professional landscaper" who landscaped those grounds, I would keep my mouth shut. Firmly shut.

In the middle of a long bowling-alley-type yard, there was a half moon cut out for a drain. One small, rather stupid looking plant was stuck next to the drain. It never grew. Never blossomed. That was it. That was the professional landscaping.

Okay. There were the stunted arbor vitae bushes between the houses. There were two rhododendron bushes under the bedroom windows. But professionally landscaped? Give me a break.

And so my faithful committee was stuck listening to me groan. Diane called and I moaned. Complained really. Groused, whined, fidgeted, and fussed. And being Diane, she called me to prayer.

"What is your heart for this yard?" she asks. "Pray for what you want."

Okay, God, I want mature landscaping. I want to look out of my windows and see a beautiful yard, crowded with your creations. I want abundance and age and style and beauty. I want a lush display of the Gardener. The Original Gardener. Now, can you fix that? How?

Today, three years later, I sit at the window of a new house. A compromise. Twenty-five years old with a good structure. Plenty of room for three growing children. Enough oddities to satisfy Carol.

Next to me, on the other side of the window, a wisteria plant is actively creeping across the railing of the deck. Lush and lovely. Behind it are two evergreens, one pine and one Douglas Fir. Both are twenty to thirty feet tall. Then there is a fig tree. Huge and beautiful, it provides shade for the bird feeder and sunbathers.

To the right is a huge willow tree. A family of squirrels lives in the fir trees behind the willow tree. My walnut tree in the front yard provides them with food. Each year at this time we are treated to their antics. They grab a walnut, run across the roof, pause at the edge and then swing through the air. Tarzan style, they grab a willow branch and swing toward the tree trunk. Then they disappear toward home. It never fails to bring all of us to the window, laughing and giggling with glee.

There is an apple tree, an ash tree, a mint plant, lilacs, star magnolias, and roses. All mature. All flowering. All wonderful.

This spring, when everything was in bloom, Diane drove over to see us. She hadn't been to this house. She did know that I loved it. And when she saw it, she cried. I had been given my heart's desire: mature landscaping.

What Diane didn't know was that the mature landscaping was a mirror of the rich spiritual place to which God had brought me through the help of many mature mentors. He had put me in the comforting place of being the child and had allowed me to learn at the feet of those who had walked longer and hiked farther with Jesus.

It would take me time to internalize all the lessons. Yet, as my classroom literally looked out on mature landscaping, I was beginning to see how God was maturing my inner landscape.

This yard is a spectacular gift to both Mark and me. We moved into this house in the dead of winter, so I had no idea about the yard. Honestly, I just wanted a family room. Not much else mattered. The owner told me it was a beautiful yard. I nodded. When we took up occupancy, she graciously left me instructions for the yard. Five or six pages of handwritten instructions. I was prepared to believe it must be some yard.

That spring our little city lot was transformed. Surprises were everywhere. Miracles. From starkness to lush fullness. I was extremely pleased. I followed her instructions to the letter. I worked hard and the rewards were endless.

In the front of the living room window sits a big green plant. It looks like all the others. Seen one plant, you've seen them all. But when this Daphne plant bloomed, it gave the entire walkway and living room a fragrance that is too sweet and too clean to capture on paper.

At Pentecost the trees that border our neighbor's yard began to bloom. Delightful pink blossoms. White flowers. And I felt wooed by the Master Gardener. Reminded that the Bridegroom created flowers for His Bride. Beautiful, fragrant blossoms. A symbol of His eternal love.

Then there is fall. Usually we have a luscious Indian Summer in Oregon. Warm days and crisp, cold nights. The flowers remain. And if they were pruned after their first bloom, many of them bloom again.

That lesson, of pruning after a bloom, is a profound one for me. Here is a lovely flower bush. In June it is decked out with gorgeous flowers. Blooms everywhere. A prettier bush cannot be found. Eventually, the bloom is over. The flowers die.

It is then the flowers need to be picked off and cut way back until the bush is no longer a lush, wild thing. Cut until there doesn't appear to be any hope for it. Cut until we are certain I must have killed it.

Then, in the early fall, the bush comes back. And miracle of miracles, it is larger and lusher than ever. The blooms are everywhere. It is without rival, a complete work of art, a masterpiece.

If the bush is not pruned after its first fruit, the bush never has the miracle of autumn. Oh, you'll get a few flowers down at the bottom, away from the dead and rotting flowers at the crest. But you will never get what should have been. The miracle is not available.

Then, after the fall flowers, you must cut the bush back again. Cut it down to the ground and give it the appearance of death. If you fail to do this, the plant will never again be beautiful. In the spring, those dead blossoms will be a home for insects who will eat any new blossoms. There will be no spring bouquets.

This simple lesson, which all gardeners are aware of, is profound. When the Lord, the Master Gardener, is at work in our lives, He must prune us. We all rejoice in the seasons when we are in full bloom. When all of the teaching and all of the prayer and all of the "fertilizing" is finished, our lives bear the unmistakable polish of fruit. Of flowers. Of visible life.

But periods of pruning are inevitable. We seldom rejoice in those. We frequently find ourselves looking at a pruned neighbor and saying, "Oh my, he must have met with failure again. Look how cut up his life is!" Then we walk away, shaking our heads and glorying that it's not us.

John 15 tells us that every branch that bears fruit is pruned back that it may bear more fruit. That means when a work of God is finished in our lives, the Master Gardener will come and cut off the work. Take it away. Get rid of the physical manifestation of it.

The process is painful. We lie exposed, vulnerable, naked. Gone are our blooms, our visible crowns. We lie dormant, in the faith that the Gardener has done the work—that the resurrection miracle of spring will come. That we really will bloom again.

I have been blessed to work a garden that someone else planted. I am reaping twenty-five years of her hard work. And I love her for it. I couldn't have planted this garden. I did not have the knowledge. So, for this season, I work in another's garden. I learn under her tutelage. And each time I am outside working in the dirt, the Master Gardener comes and teaches me little lessons.

One lesson dealt with responsibility. As so frequently happens, it was taught me by my children.

Megan, Rachael, Noah, and I do the leaves. We bag them up and give them to friends for mulch. Last year we bagged three rounds of eleven to seventeen bags. That's a lot of mulch. We got tired. We got bored. But all the while I kept thanking God for mature trees and bribing the children with promises of McDonald's.

Then Megan came to work next to me. Total innocence. "Mom, do you know about the environment?" she asked.

"Some, honey. What do you want to know?"

"Do Christians care about the environment?" she asked.

"Of course we do, Megan. Why, God made all of this beauty. We really have to be concerned. Did you know that He appointed us the caretakers of the earth? This is His garden and we are to take care of it."

Okay. I was getting high and mighty and pretty preachy. I was on a roll. My kid was going to be socially aware and responsible and…

"Mom, at school we learned how important it is to recycle. Mom, why don't you recycle?"

Gottcha. Kids really know how to aim that old guilt gun. A sure shot, my seven-year-old. Right to the center of the target.

"Uhhh…well…I guess I've never taken the time to figure the routine out. I guess I'd better get started," I groveled.

"I really think you should, Mom." Her voice was very serious. Her eyes showed their deep concern. "After all, if God made this place, aren't you responsible to Him?"

Point, set, and match to the seven-year-old.

"Yes, sweetheart. I'm responsible to Him. I guess I'd better call the city information office and find out what to do."

Then, because the Lord is sweet and forgives us, He gave us this little prayer:

> God, You made the rocks
> And You made the trees.
> You made the grass
> And You made the leaves.
> Help me be a good guardian of it.

That childish prayer has stayed with us for three years. I am about three weeks away from the great leaf job. I wonder if the children will remember it this year? I remember it. I want to learn to be a good guardian of the earth and of this little hundred-by-hundred-foot plot of ground we call home.

I am determined to learn. I can plant a bulb now. Most of my struggles really are with weeds. But I struggle with the discipline of going outdoors and playing in the land of spiders and worms. Why not leave it to Mark? Maybe *Reader's Digest* will announce I'm their sweepstakes winner, and I can hire a gardener.

Instead, I visit a friend. A master gardener. Her garden, like the rest of her home, is a work of art. She designed it; she planted it. And most important, she weeds it.

I asked her why we garden. Her reply was worth noting.

"We garden because it is a work of faith. We plant believing that these bulbs will become flowers. We water, weed, prune, and fertilize because we believe in a coming harvest, a time when all will be in bloom and the magic will return."

The next day she called. "I've been thinking about our conversation, about why we garden. You know, gardening is the first commandment. Adam and Eve were told to work the garden. It is one of the few pure commandments, prior to the Fall of man. We were created to work in a garden, to live in its magic, to understand its lessons."

A work of faith. A pure commandment. A chance to return to a place that existed prior to the Fall and to plumb its depths. True, my garden is post-Fall of man. But the lessons. The lessons are pure Jesus.

RETURNING TO THE GARDEN:

1. Read Genesis 1 and 2. List any ideas you have about what the garden was like.

2. What do you think it was like for Eve to work in the garden by day and to walk with God in the evenings?

3. Review your own yard or patio or deck. What would be your idea of Eden for this place?

4. Look through home magazines and cut out pictures of gardens and yards that appeal to you.

5. Find a friend who understands the art of gardening. Ask for help. Designate a small area of your garden as the starting place and work on it for the next six months. You can add territory once the skills are in place.

6. Purchase a small spiral notebook. Record all of the gardening lessons that mirror the lessons of the Spirit. What parables does Jesus teach you in your garden?

Holy Celebrations

*The festivities of God
fortify us against spiritual
forgetfulness.*

S. BOWEN MATTHEWS

CHAPTER EIGHT

CHRISTMAS

December 1990

Chestnuts roasting on an open fire,
Visa nipping at your nose,
Yuletide programs taking up all your nights,
And children, presents, and fights.
Everybody knows a turkey and some mistletoe,
Are the cause of Mom's exhausted sighs.
Tiny tots with their eyes all aglow,
Will never, ever sleep tonight.

I remember all those romantic dreams I had as a young person. Christmas with a lover, sleigh rides through Central Park. Perfectly dressed, well-behaved children on Christmas morning just waiting for Mommy and Daddy to hand them their presents and then saying, "No, dear sister, you open yours first."

Okay. So reality is not quite what I thought it would be. Now there are bills, Christmas programs, traffic jams, crowded stores, and midnight sessions of wrapping presents. The lover is into basketball season, not Central Park. Perfectly dressed has been translated into "anything that's clean," and the most depressing thing of all is that these beautiful children seem to have been delivered without manners. I'm sure I was born grateful. What happened to them? Must be Mark's side of the family.

Christmas is the one season that must be planned with extreme care if it is to be a time of real worship. We've all had those holidays that, while wonderful, were absolutely exhausting—Christmas celebrations that end with your sitting alone in a chair at midnight, too tired to sleep, and wondering if anyone thought about the gift of salvation at all. Or holidays that have you saying on the twentieth of December, "Only five more days to go and it's over!"

Mark and I have certainly experienced those. We have repented, planned carefully, and projected great things only to find ourselves on December 26 in bed, exhausted, reviewing how we managed to fall into the same old trap again.

Eventually the faithful committee entered. They had many things to teach us. Some of the lessons are still unpracticed—untried truths—teachings that have entered the mind but not the heart of the family. This chapter will contain only the tried truths.

Basically there are two main ingredients in our Christmases. One is planning. I plan the budget by January 1. I figure out how much Christmas is likely to cost us, add a hundred dollars to it, and still come out wrong! But it helps to be that close and to have the money taken out all year long.

We plan our December calendar as a family, agreeing on which events are keepers and which ones we will carefully omit. We also plan with our extended families in mind.

The second ingredient in our Christmases is the most important to me. We have learned, via committee member Ernestine, to select one aspect of the Christmas story on which to focus. Usually it changes from year to year. Often we think we are changing it only to find that the Lord has used new people in the story to reteach us last year's truth. One year it was the Savior baby. The next year it was the mother of Jesus. It has been lights, shepherds, the star, the relationship between Joseph and his bride, and Anna and Simeon.

Here are the stories of five different Christmases at our house. They are success stories, although I didn't think they would be when the season opened. They are family Christmases on holy ground.

CHRISTMAS 1985

One thing I'm certain of: I will never, ever have a Christmas baby. Imagine saddling a child with a birthday in December. He or she would never get a special celebration, and I believe that birthdays are very important. I want my children to have magical birthdays. Any month but December. Actually, a summer birthday would probably be best.

"Well, Mrs. Brazo. Your due date should be right around December 4, give or take a week."

I suddenly needed air. "December what?"

"December 4. But that's just a guess. Usually first babies are late. Don't worry. Sometime before the new year." Dr. Sally grinned.

I thanked this new member of the committee and quietly walked to the door. "December 4. Great. Just great. I want this child to have the best of everything, and here he or she is getting a December birthday. Well kid, you'll just have to show up a week early."

And so for seven months we make big plans. Dr. Sally makes me promise to have all Christmas shopping done, wrapped, and mailed by November 1. (This is a great practice for every year. It frees you to enjoy the month of December.) Her threat to me is that she won't be there to deliver if I don't do my homework. I am dependent on Dr. Sally. The shopping is done.

November arrives. My dear friend Cathy delivers her baby, Daniel. It wasn't an easy birth. It is her first baby too. She tells me the pain isn't really bad at all. She lied.

By November 28 I'm cheering this baby on. (I bet Mary was also rooting for an early baby—a home delivery instead of a cave in the hills of Bethlehem!) Come on, kid! You can do it!

December 1. No baby. Each day puts us closer to Christmas and further away from a "normal" birthday.

December 4. No baby.

December 7, my dad's bet. Dad thinks I would definitely choose a "day that will live in infamy!" Thanks, Dad. But no baby.

December 10. Mark's mother's birthday. A nice day for a baby. No go. Stubborn child.

December 13. "Mark, I think you should get a substitute teacher today. I feel kind of..."

Megan Jo arrives at 4:30 in the afternoon. Safely. Cathy did lie about the pain, but then this baby is worth every discomfort of the last nine months. She is perfect.

Friday the thirteenth, my personal lucky day, she weighs in at 7-11. What a fantastic kid.

The families are ecstatic. My sweet Baptist mother dances around the kitchen with the baby in her arms. Joanne and I exchange amused smiles. Mom is definitely into this "Grandma" thing.

Mark and I are supposed to teach the college class on Sunday, December 22. Never one to slow down, I dress my doll-baby up, pack a diaper bag, and go to church.

Megan is welcomed with applause. Worship takes on new meaning. Resting in my arms is seven pounds of the most precious material on earth—a child. I am overwhelmed with the vulnerability I feel. Amazed by the strength of it. Hardly able to let others hold her. Unwilling to let her out of my sight. My emotions are so fierce and yet so frighteningly fragile that I'm overpowered by them.

We sing about Mary, and I begin to understand. This Christmas, this year, we are given the unique opportunity to identify with the baby, the Savior baby, in a new way. A deep and difficult way.

Father, you sent your only son. You allowed Him to be as fragile and vulnerable as Megan. And you took this beloved One and let others raise Him, others who were not as capable as you. I can hardly let another hold my child. Other arms held your son; other voices sang to Him.

Your love is so different from mine. Mine is small, defensive, careful. Yours is enormous, free, and wild. I will never be like you. I can only worship at your feet.

Thank you. Your gift, given at this time of year, was too precious. We did not deserve such a gift. We misused your gift. And when we did, when we crucified your son, did you remember His tiny little baby feet? Did you wish you had done differently?

CHRISTMAS 1986

"No, Mrs. Brazo, it isn't a nervous breakdown. You are four months pregnant.... Due date? Well, let's see. I'd say around January 4.... Thirteen months apart? Well, Mrs. Brazo, it will all work out. You'll see."

And so I anticipate another Christmas of identification with Mary. Hugely pregnant on Christmas. Pictures from the neck up only. Two little ones, thirteen months apart.

Megan's first birthday is a huge success. The little angel is as cute as her dad thinks she is. Really. That cute. We are reminded that the season is just that, a birthday party. A huge, thirty-day birthday party.

The next morning is church. We get up, dress, and begin the drive. Ten minutes later I ask Mark to turn the car around. The next little angel is making her mama uncomfortable. Braxton Hicks contractions, I'm sure, but all the same, they hurt.

By the time we unload, I am phoning Aunt Gladys and asking her to take Megan. Just for a few hours. I'm sure it's nothing. All the same, it hurts. I want them to make it stop hurting.

We arrive at the hospital in our Sunday best. I'm in heels and navy blue hose. Elegant for this short visit.

Five hours later Rachael Joanne Brazo arrives. Safely. This time medical science is called on. Nothing hurt. Mama loves her anesthesiologist. And Rachael is the most perfect baby. Just like her sister. And yes, nurse, the charts are correct. Her sister was born a year ago yesterday. They are 366 days apart.

Families repeat the dance of celebration. Another gift has come to us. Another child from the arms of God. And she looks just like her daddy. A brown-eyed, brown-haired angel baby. We rejoice. We are overwhelmed. The emotions of a year ago are multiplied. So is the vulnerability.

Another newborn. Another visit to the heart of the Bethlehem story. And now, for the rest of my days, I will celebrate birthdays in December. Wonderful, world-changing birthdays. Children sent from God and entrusted to us. Miracles of the season.

CHRISTMAS 1990

"I'm free! I'm FREE!" Rachel's little voice proclaimed. Then, lest anyone had misunderstood her proud statement, she raised three tiny fingers to indicate her ever-so-advanced age. But I, sitting in the front seat of the van, felt my bottom lip tremble. Vision blurred as I realized this was the last time I would hear that declaration from her. Tomorrow she would be four, and I, sniffling and feeling foolish, wondered how she got to be four so fast.

Another mother, in a different age, also chronicled her child's milestones. Luke tells us she treasured these things and pondered them in her heart.

Dearest Lord, teach me to be a Mary. Teach me to record my children's triumphs. Let me remember the small things that give so much pleasure. Let me remember this Christmas as the year of the lights. You remember, Lord....

December 1—Most of those who own outdoor Christmas lights began to assemble and hang them up. As we left the house that evening, Megan, Rachael, and Noah were fascinated and delighted by them. The inevitable question was asked in high-pitched glee, "Mama, can WE have Christmas lights too?"

I did not skip a beat.

"Kids, lights are very expensive. We don't have the money in the budget for them. We need the money for other things—like bread and milk and Cheerios. Not everyone can afford lights. Remind me next summer and I will try to budget for lights. Ask Jesus to send the money for next year."

Rachael interrupted the discourse and said, "I will ask Jesus right now!" What ensued was a lengthy prayer meeting in the back of the van with each child—ages two, three, and four—asking Jesus for lights. "Pwease, Jesus. We need lights."

"Lights and bread and milk and Cheerios."

"Mommy doesn't have no money, Jesus."

"Jesus, you got to get the money, okay?"

When the last "amen" was uttered, the ever ebullient Rachael exclaimed, "Mommy! Jesus told me we would get them! This year!" I raised my eyes heavenward to remind the Lord this was not funny. "Well dear, we'll have to see."

Megan picked up the slack and explained life to her little sister. "Only rich people have lights. See those houses? Rich people live there. They have lots of lights." Then, as I turned into a different neighborhood, Megan's excitement grew. "Look, Rachael! It's okay! There are lots of poor people on this street. Only three houses have lights!"

That episode formed the foundation of our Christmas. Others heard the story, enjoyed the punch line, and donated lights. Each evening became an event as excited children danced around the switch and then watched in silent awe as the lights filled the sky.

Many profound lessons were taught me by those lights. The children reminded me that Jesus had sent us the lights, just as He had promised Rachael in the van. The lights also reminded me of His light. The dark streets reminded me that few live in the affluence of His light; most suffer in the poverty of darkness. And the children's joyful wonder reminded me of the delight found in His presence.

Rachael, tomorrow you will be four. In four years you have taught me so very much. You have reminded me time and again to treasure these things—these episodes in our lives—and to ponder them in my heart. Over and over you remind me to set aside the laundry, turn on the lights, and wonder at the holy hush that ensues.

CHRISTMAS 1991

"Wendy, can I make the three kings too?" I beg.

Wendy and Susan had just shared their plan for Monday nights this fall. They were going to sculpt three kings out of Sculpty clay and dress them up. Then, in a very Catholic tradition, they would move the kings around the house during the Advent season as the kings journeyed to find the Christ child. On Epiphany Sunday the kings come to rest at the crèche. For a child of evangelicalism, the symbolism has surpassing beauty.

By this time we had gotten into the habit of choosing a theme for each Christmas. The first year was the Savior baby, then came the year of the Savior baby's pregnant mother. There had been a celebration of light. I felt certain this year would be the kings. The symbolism was too beautiful to pass up.

Wendy and Susan laugh and agree to allow me to work with them. I am given a list of items to purchase and then told the rules.

1. You will be shown how to do this. Pay attention.
2. You will do your own work.
3. You will not quit when it gets complicated.

We agree to meet in Wendy's kitchen on Monday nights after eight o'clock. That way Susan and I can get our little ones to bed first. We will work until late. Only the Lord knows how late! I love the idea.

This year has been a difficult one for me. We have given up the children's ministry. Our vision is just too far from the church's vision. Mark is working two jobs to make ends meet. The house is up for sale. I've always disliked that house and am anxious to sell it. So far, nothing. Mark works so hard and is so exhausted. The sale of the house would allow us to move into a larger house in a lesser neighborhood and still pay off some bills.

The nights at Wendy's are a godsend. A gift to a tired Mama. A chance to be Carol instead of Mama. A much needed gift. On Monday night, materials gathered, I drive to Wendy's. It's dark and I'm tired. I'm about five minutes away from her house when my foolishness hits me.

What in the world am I doing? I've always been all thumbs. My mom is the artist. I'm the klutz. Wendy has studied sculpture at art school. She's a talented professional artist. Susan is also as artsy as they get. She can do anything, transforming junk into genius. What did I commit myself to?

The driveway is dead ahead. A choice must be made quickly. Either I chicken out and go home or I get crazy and stay. The idea of one more night at home decides me. I pull into the driveway.

Inside, the kitchen is immaculate. Wendy and Susan are there. They set up our work area at the large kitchen table. There are soft drinks and tea. Wendy's beautiful kitchen glows with soft light and classical music. My stomach begins to tighten.

"Okay. Let's get at it," Wendy commands.

"I can't tell you how I've looked forward to this," Susan says. "I've already decided how I want mine to be. I really need them to reflect worship. Worship is important to me this year. Particularly important."

They smile, contented. I smile, terrified.

I watch their actions carefully and take out my tools. I copy their moves. Finally I have the tools assembled. The clay is ready. My armpits are getting very damp. Now I will have to sculpt with my arms close to my body. Who am I fooling? It isn't like I planned to make grand sweeping motions. Honestly.

Finally we begin. We work step by step. Wendy's sculpture looks majestic. Lifelike. Real. Susan's is highly stylized. Stark. Regal. Strong.

Mine? Well, mine looks like a little old man with a big nose. A not very attractive little old man with a big nose. Kind of a caricature. Not royal. Not kingly. And certainly not majestic.

"Don't worry so much, Carol," says Wendy, smothering a laugh.

"Remember, clothes make the man. We'll dress him up and he'll look kingly."

Susan smiles encouragingly and nods. "Really. It's great. You'll see."

I smile faintly. I'm soaking wet. My stomach could use Pepto Bismol, not Diet Coke. I get up and pour another soda.

"Okay. Head number two," the staff sergeant commands.

"Really? We're still sculpting? Don't we stop and dress him, or make a body or something?" I cringe.

"Nope, head number two. Get going. It's after ten."

We all settle down at the table. Wendy is off and sculpting. Susan is also contentedly creating. I begin. No offers of help this time. Apparently the rules were for real. Oh well.

"So, Susan, I hardly know you. What is the spiritual significance of worship for you this year?" I ask.

And sweet, sincere Susan begins to share. She is completely open, and I'm enthralled with her story. The small head I'm working on is hidden in my hand. I continue to work as she continues to talk. Her story has the honest ring of authenticity. It also has the touch of the Savior woven through it.

Finally, an hour or so later, she's finished. The table grows quiet. Throughout the hour Susan and Wendy have shared their masterpieces. Mine is hidden. Worked in the circle of my arm. Hidden by my hands.

"So, Carol, are you planning to share your king with us?" Wendy asks.

"I can't!" I wail. "I messed up! And furthermore, I like the mess-up!" I feel like a five-year-old who got caught playing in the glue.

"Come on. Nothing is that bad. We can fix it," they assure me.

"But that's the problem! I don't want it fixed. It's perfect. It's just perfectly wrong. I made a woman! A little old woman. She looks like a nun," I cry.

The room explodes in laughter. It is so right. Carol makes a woman. Carol, Carol, there were no female kings.

Then they see her. The laughter dies down. While she is still primitive compared to their work, she is very precious. And she is definitely female. Even bald she is female.

Wendy is all smiles. "Maybe you weren't supposed to do kings this year. Maybe this isn't a rich year for you. Maybe the Creator had other ideas for you."

We quiet ourselves. I can't remember if we prayed aloud or silently, but prayer occurred. Then, after much quiet pondering, Wendy said, "I think maybe you are supposed to have Anna and Simeon. Maybe you were never supposed to have kings."

At that point I am too relieved to think it through. Two heads, already complete. I'm finished sculpting heads. All done. Who needs three kings if you can have Anna and Simeon? There are only two of them. Whatever the spiritual message, I'm thoroughly prepared to accept that I am to have Anna and Simeon and that I will just sit and watch them sculpt their third king's head.

Finally we pack up. I thank them and agree on the next Monday night. I drive home, stirred up, anxious. It is one o'clock when I pull into the garage.

As I sneak into bed, Mark stirs. "How'd it go?" he asks, his voice gravelly with sleep.

"Okay. It's just that I didn't get kings. I messed up and made a woman, so now Wendy thinks I should have Anna and Simeon. Maybe God has a message for me in their lives."

Mark pulls himself into an upright position. "Anna and Simeon, huh? Grab the Bible and review the story for me."

"Now, honey?" I'm incredulous.

"Yeah. If the Lord has a message for us.... Well, maybe He does," he concluded.

I found the story. Simeon and Anna. Both devoted to prayer. Both elderly. Each meets the Savior baby on His visit to the temple. The Savior is eight days old.

Anna recognizes the child on sight and praises God. Simeon takes the child in his arms and says, "My sovereign Lord. My eyes have lived to see your salvation."

Mark and I snuggle close. We need a Savior this year. A Savior to sell the house and get Mark off the two-job schedule. A Savior to help us parent. A Savior to keep Carol sane.

We smile. A Savior. A visitation of salvation. We are so in need of a Savior. So we pray, committing to meditate on Anna and Simeon this holiday season, asking God to show us His salvation in other areas of our lives.

The season approaches. The two figures are a delight. Simeon has a prayer shawl and holds a scroll with his famous words. Anna is a picture of grace. Long white hair and raised arthritic arms. A picture of praise and excitement.

I have been asked to speak at our women's Christmas dessert. Our church, in the midst of a split, needs a Savior. I will speak on Anna and Simeon and on the importance of kneeling together, at His cradle, as sisters. Regardless of our differences. Regardless of our hurts. We will seek the Savior together. We will seek healing from the Savior baby.

The Christmas dessert is to be held December 15. The house sells on December 8. I must hold two school birthday parties, find a house for us to purchase, have a family birthday party, and prepare for the dessert—in seven days. A crazy, rambling, joy of a week.

Finally the night arrives. The women come. Those who are leaving the church and those who are staying. The wounded and the intact. After we have indulged in mouthwatering cheesecake, I share, and women are invited to worship the Savior, to cry out for salvation around a rough wooden box, our version of the manger.

The response is humbling. Salvation is cried out for this church body. We beg for unity.

As it happens, this is the last time the group will worship together in this place and time. Salvation will visit us in different locations. But it will be the same Savior. And for one moment we are united at the cradle of the Savior, begging for Simeon's gift: a chance to see His salvation.

CHRISTMAS 1992

We approach this season changed people. Last year we had celebrated the Savior—salvation had come to visit us. This year we had lived to see His salvation.

One week in June Ernestine came to visit. Having laughed over the story of Anna and Simeon, she was anxious to see them. They were duly found, dusted off, and put on display. We laughed and clowned, thrilled that finally, six months after we sold the house, Mark was given a job that would fit him. A job that would allow him to quit the second job. A wonderful, sports-centered job at a high school. He would teach science and be their athletic director. Tailor-made.

We are happy in our new home, and things seem to be taking shape. After Ernestine's visit Anna and Simeon stay put. Honestly, they belonged in the attic with the other Christmas stuff, but I was just too lazy to put them away.

Vacation Bible School begins, and Noah opts to stay with Mom. As we leave the church that morning, Noah has a question. "Mom, will I be fat like you when I grow up?"

Talk about quenching the spirit. He asked in total innocence, a three-year-old trying to see what to expect. I went home, cried my eyes out, and found that book I'd been avoiding, The Love Hunger Workbook. Cursed thing. It begins with the acknowledgment that Carol's life, my life, is out of control and that I need a Savior. I begin the work.

Same month. Mark is up to new tricks. Seeing stacks of journaling paper litter my desk, he finally gets an inspiration. After making a few calls, he signs a check and informs me he has signed me up for a writer's conference. Everything inside me panics. I can't write! Journaling is one thing, but real writing?

Friends sign up to baby-sit the kids. Mom and Dad encourage me. Wendy arrives with a coloring book and crayons; she claims they are therapeutic and that unless one enters as a little child...

I attend the conference in a fragile state of wonder. Here are two hundred people who think as strangely as I do. They're as crazy as I am. And some of them are paid for it! Mark was right. This may well be my country of spiritual origin.

This year, by August 15, we are certain we will study the shepherds. They also see Salvation and fall to worship Him. They hear heavenly voices and are courageous enough to explore their promise. The year we have spent exploring the promises of salvation has been a wild adventure, taking us on journeys we never expected. Now we will honor other adventurers. Shepherds.

There's a problem. There is no record of female shepherds. I have two small daughters. I am determined they not think that the exciting, life-giving events of Scripture were for men only. And so we begin to pray. I sculpt shepherds out of clay. I costume them. But I need a woman in the story.

And then one day a story begins to form. The Lord gives me a delightful story for my children. It is the story of a family of shepherds and their daughter Esther. Esther is the youngest in a family of daughters, and as such, she has to tend the family sheep. Her cousins tease her, and only her uncle Josiah recognizes her sensitive little soul. Each night the Creator told her stories of the beginnings, and each night Esther was resouled. The story takes them from the hills of Bethlehem to a crowded little cave and a newborn King. There Esther holds Salvation Himself in her seven-year-old arms.

The story is written. The lessons are learned. I weigh fifty pounds less, Mark has a wonderful new job, and each of us has held salvation closer than ever before. Salvation in one's embrace...what a concept.

❖

As you approach this holiday season, read and meditate on the story of His birth. Read Matthew 1-2; Luke 1-2; John 1:1-14; Isaiah 7:14 and 9:6-7; Daniel 2:44-45 and 7:14.

1. Whose story interests you the most? Mary's, the Babe's, Joseph's, the angels', the shepherds', Elizabeth's, the prophets'?

2. What was it like to be in their shoes? What was it like to prophesy something you never lived to see?

3. How can you use the stories of these people or things to build your Christmas? As decor? In your devotions? In your gift-giving?

4. How can you teach your children the truths found in their stories?

5. What one aspect of their stories has a lesson for your own life?

6. Spend some time in prayer, committing yourself to learn the lessons their stories can teach you.

7. Set aside specific time to teach your family the truths you are learning.

8. On November 15 sit down as a family and agree on a December calendar of family events. Remember, more is not better. Guard your time, lest you find yourself celebrating Christmas without worshiping the Christ.

WINTER

July 1984

Dear God, why is this happening to us? Why are you silent? Have we in any way offended you? Are we at fault?

In May we felt your leading. We knew we should return to southern California. Because of the problems of the last year, I was not anxious to return. But your leading was so strong. Everyone agrees. You want us here.

Then in June Mark goes in for a physical. They find a lump. Exploratory surgery with major consequences if the lump is malignant. Four days we live in a silent no-man's-land. You send precious little reassurance. The only verse that is capable of sustaining us is "Lo, I am with you always." That provides some comfort, but it doesn't tell me that Mark will be free of cancer. I feel such fear. We haven't even been married a year.

This year of marriage has been too good. We adjusted to living together in about five minutes. The joy of constantly being together is overwhelming. The ability to make love and know it is not only sanctioned by you but celebrated by you is a miracle. A wonderful, joyful miracle. It has been a year of excessive happiness.

And then this. I can't begin to think about losing Mark. We have become so wedded in one year that the thought you might take him now is obscene.

Finally the day comes. Surgery is done. Scar tissue removed. No cancer. Apparently a boy of eight snapped a towel at my husband back in 1962, and the resulting scar tissue has put us through a week of hell. And Mark will spend several weeks recovering.

Mark is adamant that we go ahead with the move. Armed with ice packs and pain pills, we kiss everyone good-bye and head south. Mark's father has also had a cancer scare this month. A spot on his nose is malignant. Skin cancer. It is removed while Mark is in surgery. Success. No need for further treatment.

We arrive in L.A. and move into Mark's parents' home where we will stay until August. Then teaching jobs will allow us to move into our own home. Everything has been lovingly prepared for our stay. We will live in Mark's old bedroom. The idea is rather fun.

Mom and Dad come to L.A. to spend July 4 with the entire Brazo clan. Then Ruth and Luke, Mark's mother and father, head for June Lake for fishing, and we stay and entertain my parents. Five days later, as we are leaving for a Dodger baseball game, the phone rings. It's Ruth. Luke has died of a heart attack. He had fished all morning and slept all afternoon. Sometime during that nap, you had come and taken him home to your house.

All the pressure and darkness that surrounded us only two weeks ago return in full force. Mark is an amazing man. He goes to his room and weeps. I follow him and wrap him in my arms. He's crying out to you. Thanking you for his father. Thanking you for a swift and painless death. Begging for help. But mostly thanking you. What kind of man am I married to? How does a person spend grieving time in thanksgiving? Thanksgiving washed with tears of profound grief.

Ruth and Luke had been married forty years. How will she cope? We will stay through September.

All the while you are silent. I can see why you sent us here. I just don't understand. This is so very hard. We are so miserable.

I have only been part of this family for one year. I have seen them maybe fifteen or twenty times. I hardly know them. And we are being forced to operate as a family on some major issues. Luke was the only one I felt totally relaxed with. Now what?

Where are you? I need help.

Winter times. Those amazingly difficult times in life when God seems as removed as the daffodils. As silent as the falling snow. Those seasons of life that we would prefer to live without.

The first real spiritual winter I remember came at the end of my first year of marriage. Surgery for Mark, a homecoming for Luke, a difficult year in Los Angeles. It was a time of deep grief. A time of testing. A time of silence.

The God who turned water into wine had moved on to the God of Gethsemane. It was an experience I will never forget. It was so hard to suffer His silence and remain convinced that I had not failed Him in some way.

Just before Mark's surgery a committee member contacted me. She had been praying for me and felt compelled—even pushed—to give me a book. And she was embarrassed. She knew us. She knew that our brand-new marriage was a treasure to us, that we were in newlywed heaven. Nevertheless, she was being commanded to pass on to me a book about pain, where the two guides are sorrow and suffering.

Hinds Feet on High Places came into my possession. I wasn't sure what I needed this book for, but it was well written and fun to read. I like analogies, and so the book was pleasant company. Interesting concept, learning to follow Jesus by embracing sorrow and suffering. Interesting, but not very compelling. Not anything I wanted to go looking for.

Then came the weeks following Luke's death, painful weeks of adjustment. Of Mark being needed by a larger family. Of Mark working through pain and grief. The temperature in Los Angeles that summer was smothering. We suffered physically, emotionally, and spiritually.

We had no church. Mark's family church was not what we were looking for. Chuck Smith at Calvary Chapel was a joy, but an hour away. And it was large. Very large. We knew we needed a small church body that would take us in and love us through a difficult season.

No such body was found. We looked for an entire year. Every Sunday morning Mark teased, "These are the voyages of the starship Brazo on its one-year quest to find a church." The starship was destined to circle planets and never land. Seldom were we even allowed to beam down for a closer look. Spiritual loneliness added to our grief.

The committee remained in touch by phone and letter. The books sent my way are my treasures. Jesse Penn Lewis, C. S. Lewis, Hannah Whitall Smith, and Hannah Hurnard kept me. They literally kept me. Their words and the spirit of their words were my vanguards, my protection against the ever-widening abyss.

The rehearsing of Scripture, memorizing and meditating, became more than important. It became a lifeline. It taught me what to expect and how to hang on. When England alone stood in the gap against Nazi Germany, Winston Churchill said, "Wars are not won by evacuations." I determined that I might not like what I saw in my life, but I would not evacuate the faith that had kept me thus far. I would just endure the war.

Here again Scripture instructed me. Hebrews 10:35-39 gave me backbone. "So do not throw away your confidence; it will be richly rewarded. You need to persevere so that when you have done the will of God, you will receive what he has promised. For in just a very little while, 'He who is coming will come and will not delay. But my righteous one will live by faith. And if he shrinks back, I will not be pleased with him.' But we are not of those who shrink back and are destroyed, but of those who believe and are saved."

So I would persevere. I would not just endure. I would fight the good fight. And for the first time in my adult life, I knew the fight was on.

Equipping oneself for battle was another lesson from Scripture. Ephesians 6:10-18 outlined the weapons of war and the armor of God. It helped, and it also led me to other passages. I had been instructed to use the sword of the Spirit, which is the Word of God. I returned to other sections of that Word.

I looked first for a promise, something similar to the song that speaks of beauty for ashes. I found it in Hosea 2:15: "There I will give her back her vineyards, and will make the Valley of Achor a door of hope. There she will sing as in the days of her youth, as in the day she came up out of Egypt."

A door of hope. Singing. I love the imagery.

As soon as I had a vision of where we were headed in this season of sorrow and loneliness—headed toward a door of hope, a place where we would sing youthfully—I started hunting for scriptures that would keep me focused and would help my belief system grow stronger. No surprises here. Scripture had what I needed.

Colossians 3:16 admonished me, "Let the word of Christ dwell in you richly."

Psalm 1:2 said that my "delight is in the law of the Lord, and on his law [she] meditates day and night."

First Thessalonians 5:16-18 told me to be thankful in all circumstances. I had seen Mark sobbing out his thanks to God. It was a new picture of thanksgiving. Not the standard one of the child's being given her heart's desire and rushing to the parent to thank him. This one showed the child crying out in pain and yet thanking the Father for His care and provision. This unexercised muscle would take time to develop.

Hebrews 12:28 said, "Therefore, since we are receiving a kingdom that cannot be shaken, let us be thankful, and so worship God acceptably with reverence and awe." *A kingdom that cannot be shaken. Thankfulness as a form of worship. A sacrifice of praise.* In this season of winter, all praise was a sacrifice. It cost me something to lay aside my grief and despair and to thank God. To worship Him.

Today, the Song of Songs keeps me: "I opened for my lover, but my lover had left; he was gone. My heart sank at his departure. I looked for him but did not find him. I called him but he did not answer. The watchmen found me as they made their rounds in the city. They beat me, they bruised me; they took away my cloak, those watchmen of the walls! O daughters of Jerusalem, I charge you—if you find my lover, what will you tell him? Tell him I am faint with love" (5:6-8). One of the earmarks of a spiritual winter is a silence on the part of God. We look earnestly and seem unable to find Him.

Finally, the daughters of Jerusalem ask the bride what manner of person is her beloved. These words, after the lament, are healing words. They lift the spirit above the happenings of the day and infuse the spirit with the reality of who He is. "My lover is radiant and ruddy, outstanding among ten thousand. His head is purest gold; his hair is wavy and black as a raven. His eyes are like doves by the water streams, washed in milk, mounted like jewels. His cheeks are like beds of spice yielding perfume. His lips are like lilies dripping with myrrh. His arms are rods of gold set with chrysolite. His body is like polished ivory decorated with sapphires. His legs are pillars of marble set on bases of pure gold. His appearance is like Lebanon, choice as its cedars. His mouth is sweetness itself; he is altogether lovely. This is my lover, this my friend" (5:10-16).

Fixing my eyes on Jesus, the author and finisher of our faith, keeps me. It provides a steadying hand. I find myself able to stand a bit firmer if I stop and admire my beloved. Scriptural glimpses of the Eternal Bridegroom have become a haven for me. A place to come and restore balance. A place that reminds me who is in control.

In winter times the inspired Word of God and the writings of saints who have gone before are the difference between life and death. When I've been certain I could not survive another day in that chilly spiritual season, the words of the bride in the Song of Songs call me back. They remind me of who He is. And that He eventually does find her.

Winter in the state of Oregon is also a dreary time. We seldom have snow; rain, sleet, and ice seem to be the standards. It's dark by half past four in the afternoon. The days are short and the light is clouded.

We use those months to teach our children about the winter of the soul— those seasons where the Life-Giver seems far off. Those time periods where all that is good and brimming with life lies hidden and dormant. The years of the Israelites in the wilderness.

We teach our children by bringing into the house the signs of winter. The excesses of Christmas are put away, and the decor of the house is stark. We live with few items of beauty instead of walls and walls of beauty. Toys are sorted, and only two or three are left out; the others go to the attic. This is an excellent way to preserve Christmas presents. The bulk of them go away and then can be reintroduced over the next several months. That way each toy gets its time in the sun as opposed to all toys being trashed within three months.

The lavish food of the holidays is a memory, and we enter a period that has fewer desserts, less sour cream, and little red meat. Our bodies have indulged, and it is good to put away the excess and concentrate on being happy with less. We deliberately experience the joy of leaving the dinner table while we still feel good, and we rediscover vegetables in their natural state.

It's an excellent time to play with jigsaw puzzles. Winter seasons in our lives are always puzzling, and working puzzles with the children begins to teach them that it's hard to see the entire picture when only the frame has been filled in. It teaches trust that a good and wonderful picture will emerge ultimately.

And periodically in Oregon, winter creates a land of magic, a land covered with snow. Because snow comes only a few times each year, we awake to wonder. We are quieted by it, soothed by its beauty. Yet excited by the prospect of sledding and snowmen. Anxious to make hot chocolate.

The beauty of the snow is a reminder of the Savior. Even in times of winter, when all around us appears dead and broken, He is capable of coming when we least expect it. Of leaving beauty for ashes. Of promising resurrection. Of overcoming. Of victory.

And so we celebrate physical winter in the hope that when the spiritual winter overtakes us again, we will be ready. We will be shored up by memories of snow. Made strong by the discipline of fasting. Able to endure with the promise of a finished puzzle, a coming resurrection.

As you approach the next winter season, think about the winters of your own spiritual life. Take these months to learn how to endure these times. Find physical ways to practice spiritual lessons in your own home.

PART ONE

Choose one or two of the following individuals and study their lives: Job, Peter, Paul, Ruth, Sarah, Mary, Naomi, Hannah, and Elizabeth. How did they deal with harsh seasons? Did they live to see a resurrection? Was their hope destroyed? Did they find a door of hope? Did they sing again?

PART TWO

Design physical activities to do with your children from January to March. You might begin with these ideas.

• Put puzzles together.

• Go on treasure hunts to see if they can find God's hidden beauty in a barren landscape.

• Teach them the stories of Job, Ruth, Naomi, and others. Acquaint them with the truth that this is a hard and difficult world. Then show them the wonder of the Savior in the midst of a dry and weary land.

• Rent *The Hiding Place* for older children.

• Help out at a church soup kitchen, which children of all ages will benefit from.

Let your children become aware, while still under your protection, that there can be difficult times in life. Then strengthen their faith in God's ability to leave beauty in the wake of difficulty.

CHAPTER TEN

LENT

May 1990

I do not understand things. Many things. One thing in particular puzzles me—Easter. Why do Christians go all out at Christmas (when it seems to me that Mary did the majority of the work) and ignore Easter? Why don't we have a thirty-day party for the redeeming work of Christ? At our church we're lucky if it lasts a week. This does not feel right to me. Could it be that we identify with Mary and giving birth, so Christmas is more comfortable for us? Certainly none of us identifies with raising from the dead. No one I know anyway.

One friend said it was a "Protestant thing." The Catholics have Lent, and the Protestants protest. And here is where I made my big mistake. I decided that at least the Catholics did something, so that something must be for me. I determined to "do Lent."

I'll never forget my search for the holy in Lent. First, I informed God of my decision. I told Him that Lent involved forty days of fasting. (Later I learned that I did not have even this detail right!) I told God I would fast from all desserts. I also told Him that I needed to lose weight and I hoped we could make the whole thing mesh. (Okay, I, too, cringe at the presumption, but I want to be really honest. I wanted the two to help each other along. Talk about the negative aspects of immaturity!)

So I went off and "did Lent."

Not surprisingly, it was a disaster. A dear friend took me to an Ash Wednesday service. I dressed up. I got quiet inside. I expected to find Jesus. I expected a holy meeting with my Lord.

The ceremony was beautiful—the kneeling, the sign of the cross. The stations of the cross were explained to me, and they touched my evangelical soul to its roots. I was all prepared for an invitation into His courts.

The priest called us forward and, making the sign of the cross on our foreheads, said, "Remember thou art dust, O man, and to dust thou wilt return." He had hundreds of people to anoint. His voice, working hard to fulfill his office, took on the cadence of an auctioneer. I was devastated. Disappointed to my toes. I saw people who were so serious and others who were so vacant.

That night I poured out my heart to the Lord. I told Him of my disappointment. And He answered. He reminded me that "Man looks at the outward appearance, but the LORD looks at the heart" (1 Samuel 16:7). I was making judgments that weren't mine to make. If I had failed to find the holy in Ash Wednesday, might it not be that I was looking at others and expecting them to be my ticket to the holy place? Had I spent my own time at the foot of the Savior? People can never take the place of Jesus. No pastor, priest, or rector can compare to the guidance of the Holy Spirit. They are important; they can and do teach us. But they are not our Savior. I had ignored my Lord.

I must admit, this Easter got past me. What started out with such good intentions ended in failure. On Easter Sunday I wrote these words:

> *Dear Lord, I am not very happy. I look back over these pages and realize this past Easter was another failure. I promised you I would fast and leave out desserts. I was ready to be sacrificial. Lord, I gained five pounds. I don't think I skipped a single dessert.*
>
> *Today was another mad dash to get hats and gloves, diaper bags and Easter baskets. Once there, the music was stirring, the sermon impressive. But my spirit was flat. I feel flat...fat and flat. I didn't worship in the way I had planned.*
>
> *I'm just a fat failure.*

This time of spiritual flatness turned out to be one of those priceless lessons. It suddenly hit me that I had decided to do Lent. I had decided to work up a system to worship God. I never asked God what act of worship He desired. I just made decisions and informed Him of them.

I had confused our roles. I needed to ask God what act of worship He desired. He would give me the format. Then I would be able to worship in the true sense.

And once the lesson was solid, I felt His overwhelming peace and approval. He knew how I longed for His courts. He would bring wonderful resurrection celebrations to our house. We would just be careful to let Him design them next time.

Easter returned, one year later. In the time it took to reappear, the Lord had begun to work in my life. I asked Him about Lent. I went to the Ash Wednesday service—the same service, same church, same priest. But it was a different Carol who attended. The holy time in His courts I had longed for a year ago became my experience that night. I had been studying Ecclesiastes, especially chapter 5. "Do not be quick with your mouth, do not be hasty in your heart to utter anything before God. God is in heaven and you are on earth, so let your words be few."

I kept my eyes on Him. I heard His admonition to remember my place in His kingdom. I remembered that I was made of dust and destined to return to it. I also reveled in the knowledge that He loved that dust and had died to secure it everlasting life.

THE EASTER TREE

By this time I had studied Lent. I learned that it is a time period modeled after the forty days Christ fasted in the desert prior to being tempted by Satan. It is a time set aside to look at God's call on our lives, to reflect and recommit to our own unique mission established by God, to review our commitments and obligations. It is practiced by Christians of various denominations. Mark and I loved the idea.

During that Easter my artist friend, Wendy, decided to do an Easter tree to teach her children about God's covenant to His people. She would trace His promise, beginning with creation and ending at the empty tomb. She would trace His faithfulness and His children's unfaithfulness. Each night John and she would teach the children the biblical story, and then they would put an ornament on the tree to represent the story. She would begin the tree on Ash Wednesday and finish it the Monday after Easter.

Listening to Wendy tell about it stirred something deep within me. I knew she was on holy ground. I asked if she would mind if I made my own Easter tree.

Ever a wise woman of God, she replied, "No. I think it would be great. It's just that I can't help you with the ornaments. You need to forge this one alone with Jesus; otherwise it's just Carol feeding off Wendy's spiritual experience. I'll give you the forty stories I'm using, and you may use them as a guide."

I knew I could prayerfully choose forty Bible stories to teach His faithfulness. But designing forty ornaments to represent His faithfulness was another story.

"Okay," I stammered. "Umm...Wendy?" My voice got tiny. "Do you think you could tell me if I'm crazy once I decide on the ornaments? You know, tell me if the task is beyond me? Help me to scale down to my level? Could you please, Wendy?" I felt like a small child asking the president of the United States to help me with an essay on the Constitution. My hands were sweaty and my eyes wide.

"Of course, Carol." Her voice was soft and gentle. "That I can help with. Do you understand I'm not trying to hide anything from you? It's just that if it is to be real for your family, you must seek out the Savior on your own." She smiled.

I smiled too. Wendy can take garbage from my garage and make it look as if it came from the Louvre. Wendy had no idea how bad my art work could get. I knew. I smiled out of politeness.

She smiled out of knowledge. She knew her Creator and she knew His power. She sensed that her funny little friend was about to be invited on a date with the Savior. She had been on several such dates and knew that no one returns unloved, unaffirmed, or unhappy. Joy was just around the corner.

The following letters from my prayer journal tell the most amazing tale, the tale of a frantic child convinced of her inabilities and an awesome God who lovingly dealt with her and her family in ways they never expected.

Dear Lord, I am having the most fun! This Easter tree is just a total gas. Last night we took a short log that would stand stolidly alone and drilled a hole into it. In it we dropped a mustard seed and explained to the children about faith. Tonight we will put a branch from the walnut tree into it and discuss your role as the vine and ours as the branches.

Tomorrow night the game is afoot. A tiny toy globe with a plastic dove glued atop will represent Creation. It is wrapped in pretty tissue paper, and after we tell the children the story of Creation, one of them will unwrap the ornament and tie it to the tree. An apple will represent the Fall of man—hardly original, but after all, you're dealing with me! A Noah's ark ornament will represent the Flood. For Abraham and Sarah I have a picture of an old man and old woman holding hands. Twigs and a toy knife tied together will represent Isaac. That takes care of this week!

Thank you, Jesus. The children are very excited, and so are Mark and I. I love you.

Then I felt such overwhelming peace. It was as if He had said, "Happy Easter, Carol Jo."

Dear Lord, we are having such a blast. Each morning the children spend breakfast reminding me that we must do the "twee" tonight. Megan is old enough to guess which stories come next.

Lord, I have a bit of a challenge this week. I need to find a ladder for Jacob, a burning bush for Moses, a Passover lamb, something that will represent the judges of Israel, an anointing horn for Samuel, and an ornament for King David. This is really exciting. It's like going on a treasure hunt for adults. I'm having such fun.

Thank you, Father. Thank you for this wonderful time around your Word. Thank you for the creative pleasure. Thank you for the delight it brings to the children. Thank you for Mark's willingness to jump in and teach the stories to the children. This feels so right. It feels like a real family.

Thank you.

Dearest Lord, this is really an amazing adventure. Today we went to the fabric store, and they had some small charms for decorations. The salesperson actually got into the game of looking for the right ornament. She found a crown for the kings and a harp for David.

Jesus, this is a comfortable way to share you. I have no problems asking for help with my tree. I explain carefully what I am doing and am still amazed at the response. People are so willing to have the individual story told to them so they can help me find an ornament. They get into it and are at least as determined as I am.

Thank you. We found a plastic bush for Moses and a stuffed lamb for Passover. We glued together two pieces of wood and made a gavel for the judges. The toy ladder off Noah's fire truck became Jacob's ladder. Pretty beads glued together formed Samuel's horn of anointing, and we have the crown and harp for the kings and David. Amazing. Even Wendy is impressed!

Dear God, this is really a monumental task. This week I will need a temple for Solomon, something that represents the prophets, a wall for Nehemiah, a chain for the years of slavery, something to represent four hundred years of silence on your part, and ornaments for the annunciation and birth of Jesus. Not an easy week.

Lord, I need your help. Wendy is so generous with her ideas and so creative. I will seek her assistance if I have to, but more than anything I need your assistance, your touch. I want these ornaments to be from you—not just an exercise in creativity. Please, Jesus, please send pictures to us.

Dearest Lord, it's UNREAL! I can't believe you! You must have just sat back and laughed. Here I was worrying, and you had planned the most profound week of all.

By Saturday afternoon I was really beginning to sweat. I needed a temple for Solomon by Sunday. With dragging feet I trudged into the last untapped craft store in the Pacific Northwest.

The guy at the register was positively chipper. I was not.

"How can I help you?" he asked in a lilting voice.

My voice did not lilt. "Uhhh...I'm working on this project. It's an Easter tree to teach my children about God's covenant with man. I need an ornament for Solomon's temple." It was a textbook recital. No excitement on my part. No awe. No wonder.

"A what tree?"

"An Easter tree. Look," I said, wanting to pick up the pace, "do you have anything that might represent a temple?"

This guy was a definite conqueror. The quest for the grail was on.

"Okay. A temple. What did this temple look like?"

"Well, it was large, gold, and ornate. But this just needs to be an approximation. Just a picture to go with the story. But it needs to be three dimensional so that it can hang on a branch."

"Gold? Silver?" he asked, his hands already searching shelves.

"Gold would be good." I began to feel as if I had come to the right place.

The store was two stories. We traversed its entire floor space and came up empty.

"Okay. Here's how it is," he said. "We're going to have to build this ornament from scratch. I'll get the tag board and the pillars and paint." And before I could respond, he was gone.

Returning he said, "Glue these together and spray them gold. It will look great. By the way, does anything go in this temple?"

"Well yes, actually. I had hoped to put a piece of purple fabric lying on the floor to represent the torn veil."

"Torn veil? What was that about?"

And that began a very quiet time of me explaining to this nice young man about the Holy of Holies. I explained how the veil separated man from God. I explained how only the priest could enter the Holy of Holies and only on special days. Then I told him of your redemption and how, as you breathed your last, the veil was torn from top to bottom.

When I finished, there was silence. Serious brown eyes found my blue ones. He smiled faintly and murmured, "It's a beautiful story."

"It was a beautiful act," I agreed.

"I'm so glad you told me that story," he said.

Lord, I'm not an evangelist. I didn't know how to continue, and, honestly, it didn't seem appropriate. He had turned to ring up my purchases, and new customers were coming in.

Such a tiny touch. Such a simple story. But Jesus, you do so love that young man. Bring someone else along to reap the harvest. He loved your story. He will love you too.

Dear Lord, today I was frantic for an ornament for the prophets of God. I walked into a gift shop, told the attendant my problem, and the game continued.

"Prophets? What did prophets do actually?" she asked, all professional and stuffy.

Regretting my question, I replied in a soft voice, "They heard God's voice and spoke His word to the people."

"We'll need something a bit more concrete than that," she said in a reproving tone. "Did any of them lead exceptional lives?" Her tone was brisk. She clearly wanted to finish with me and get on to other things.

"Actually, all of them did. One called down fire from the sky, one left this life by riding on a chariot into the sky, and then there was Jonah. He ended up in the belly of a whale."

"A whale? Great. Got just the thing." And off she walked only to return with a small glass ornament of a whale. Perfect.

As she rang up the sale, her face softened. "I hadn't thought about the prophets of God in a long time," she said.

"They were a rather amazing group," I replied. "Thank you so much for finding my whale. I'll think of you each year when it is hung on the tree," I promised.

"Thank you. It was Jonah? Jonah and the whale?"

"Yes, it was Jonah." Quietly I left the store.

God, why is Jonah of interest to her? Did she once hear your voice and choose to ignore you? She does have a soft heart. I realize it's covered up with all kinds of disguises, but she, too, likes your stories. Jesus, send other people with better words than mine. Let them tell her more of your stories.

Dear Lord, an amazing week. Chain from the hardware store represents the years of bondage. Wendy taught me how to build a wall of clay for Nehemiah. A Christmas angel will represent the annunciation, and a picture of a mother and child will be for your birth.

Wendy came up with the most profound ornament for the four hundred years of silence. We made miniature scrolls, rolled them up tight, and glued a lock on them. Your words were under lock and key. Then we hung a small moon from the bottom of the scroll to represent "spiritual night"—a time when your voice was silent. My children may not understand that ornament well, but it is really for Mark and me.

Lord, please continue to speak to us. Please keep your word open and available to us. Don't let us suffer a four-hundred-year silence.

Bless Wendy. She is such a gift. A kindred spirit. A joy. Thank you for creating a Wendy.

Dear Lord, this week is a bit easier. I found a wonderful bead shop in downtown Portland and stocked up. I have a pyramid to represent your boyhood in Egypt. I have a rubber grasshopper to represent John the Baptist. I have a dove for your baptism and a snake wrapped around a cactus for your period of temptation. I found a silk lily to represent your teaching and a tiny basket with goldfish for your miracles. I got brave and made a man out of Sculpty clay for Lazarus and then wrapped him in graveclothes. We are all set.

Lord, these evenings with the children are so meaningful to me. Their questions are amazing. They want to know why you came as a baby. When I found baby pictures of the children later that night, it struck me. Everyone loves a baby. No one is scared of a baby. Jesus, if you had come as the King of Kings and Lord of Lords, that would have scared people! Instead you came as a vulnerable, love-hungry child, and we were unafraid. Tonight I will tell them why I think you came as a baby.

Dear Lord, we are ready for Passion Week. This week we have a palm for Sunday and spilled coins for Monday. Tuesday is a scroll for your teaching, and Wednesday is a checklist for Passover, hanging from the mouth of a lamb. Thursday is the cup and the bread. Friday is the cross. Saturday is silent. Sunday is the empty tomb. The children made it from clay.

Please be present. We have done this for thirty-some days now. Don't let it become routine just when it should be climactic.

Dear Father, last night it came to me that I was forgetting something. The marriage supper of the Lamb. The last part of the covenant, as yet unfulfilled. I will make a place mat with gold silverware, and we will teach the children about the promise to come.

Dear Lord, here it is—Easter tree, year two. The children are clamoring for it and we are all excited. I'm thrilled that I have very little work to do with it this year. I also want to share it with others who may be in our home over Sabbath celebrations.

Lord, are we supposed to do it again?

Dear Lord, Wendy had an unbelievable experience this week. An artist friend came to visit and saw the tree on her kitchen counter. One thing led to another, and pretty soon they were out on the porch and Wendy was allowed to go through the entire tree, teaching you.

When she finished, the woman was in tears. "No one ever explained God to me like this. I never knew He cared so much. I never knew," she cried. She sobbed in Wendy's arms and then invited you into her life.

Lord, I am so amazed at the power of this tree. It seems so many have never heard your story. Pictures and ornaments make sense to them, and they begin to see. Thank you for speaking to each of us in a language we can understand. I always did love picture books.

Dear Lord, sheep and lambs. I spent the day with children and sheep and lambs. Lord, I am profoundly moved by the pictures of sheep and lambs. When you entered Jerusalem as a child and heard the bleating of the sheep, did you know that one day you would be that sacrificial lamb?

Later Wendy and I drove over to Marcy's house. It's her first year to try an Easter tree, so she is doing just a few ornaments. She took us into her kitchen and began to show us her ornaments. "I know they are nothing like yours or Carol's," she told Wendy.

"Marcy…," Wendy wailed. (Older sisters always wail.) "Marcy, the whole point is for you to find your own expressions."

"I know that. Anyway. I wanted you to see these two ornaments," Marcy said.

In her hand sat two small ornaments. One was rice you throw at a wedding, wrapped in tulle and tied with small ribbons and two rings. The other was a similarly shaped, small leather bag that had coins coming out of it.

"Do you see?" she asked.

I did not see. Sometimes the simplest truth is beyond me.

"They look the same. They are the same shape and the same size, but one of them represents the Bride of Christ, and one of them represents the betrayer of Christ. I hadn't planned them. They just happened this way. I'm amazed at their similarities. Then I began to realize that the disciples had not understood that Judas was the betrayer, because he looked just like them. I began to wonder if I looked more like the bride or the betrayer," she concluded.

An awestruck silence filled the kitchen. Outside the children squealed and laughed. Inside the big children spent time at your feet. Do I look like the bride or the betrayer, Lord? I want to be the bride so badly. Dress me in your robes of righteousness. I have none of my own to wear.

Today we are in a church that celebrates Lent. We still do the Easter tree and love it, but this year we added the "Ashes to Easter" small-group study to our schedule. This allowed us to meet with other adults and look at the symbols of the Gospels—water, bread, fire, salt, the cross—and how they relate to each of us. The last week of Lent was dedicated to services that included a forty-eight-hour "watch and pray" period from Maundy Thursday at nine (Last Supper) until Easter morning. (Okay, more than forty-eight hours!)

Whatever you choose to do, set aside the time. Recognize the significance of the work of Christ. Set aside forty days and review it. Think about it, talk about it, teach your children of it, and learn from it. That work was pivotal for the history of the human race. Don't let a busy schedule demean it.

Easter trees can seem like a wonderful idea until you sit down to design and create forty individual ornaments! Many families who have adopted the idea started by making one ornament per week for the six weeks of Lent and then added the seven ornaments of Holy Week. Others have done only the Holy Week ornaments, and still others have done one for each week of Lent and one for Holy Week.

The exciting thing about starting small is that each ornament is given the family's full attention. Every year the family can add new ornaments, and Mom does not need to feel that the producing of Easter tree ornaments has taken over her life!

These are the ornaments I would chose to start an Easter tree the first year.

WEEK ONE

The Fall of Man—Genesis 3. An apple or something to represent Adam and Eve or the serpent.

WEEK TWO

Passover—Exodus 12. A lamb.

WEEK THREE

Samuel anoints David—1 Samuel 16. Two beads glued together to form a horn.

WEEK FOUR

The baptism of Jesus—Luke 3. A dove.

WEEK FIVE

Sermon on the Mount—Matthew 5-7. A miniature lamp.

HOLY WEEK

Sunday: Palm Sunday—Matthew 21. A palm branch.

Monday: Cleansing the temple—Mark 11. A whip.

Tuesday: Jesus anointed—John 12. A small beaded box.

Wednesday: Judas plots—Matthew 26. A bag with silver coins.

Thursday: The Last Supper—Luke 22. A loaf of bread and a cup.

Friday: Crucifixion—Luke 23. A cross.

Saturday: Mystery Saturday—1 Peter 3:18-22. No ornament.

Sunday: HE IS RISEN!—Mark 16. A clay tomb—empty.

Monday: The marriage supper of the Lamb—Revelation 19. A place mat with gold silverware.

If, however, you want to create an ornament for the entire forty-two days, here are suggestions to get you started:

Day 1: Faith—Matthew 17:20. Have a hollowed out log and bare branch from a tree. Drill a hole in the log and put a mustard seed in it. Place the branch in the hole so that it resembles a small tree.

Day 2: Creation—Genesis 1. A small globe with a dove glued on top

Day 3: The Fall—Genesis 3. An apple or something to represent Adam and Eve or the serpent.

Day 4: Noah and the Flood—Genesis 6-9. An ark ornament or an animal.

Day 5: Abraham and Sarah—Genesis 12. A picture of a farming couple or a star ornament to illustrate the covenant.

Day 6: Abraham and Isaac—Genesis 22. Twigs tied together with a plastic knife tied on top.

Day 7: Jacob and Esau—Genesis 27. An ornament of twins.

Day 8: Jacob's ladder—Genesis 28. A toy fire truck ladder.

Day 9: Joseph—Genesis 37. A coat of many colors.

Day 10: Moses—Exodus 3. A bush.

Day 11: Passover—Exodus 12. A lamb.

Day 12: Ten Commandments—Exodus 20. A cardboard version of the tablets.

Day 13: The Judges—Judges. A courtroom gavel.

Day 14: Israel desires a king—1 Samuel 8. A coat-of-arms patch.

Day 15: Samuel anoints David—1 Samuel 16. Two beads glued together to form a horn.

Day 16: David as musician—Psalms. A golden harp.

Day 17: Solomon—1 Kings 7-9. A cardboard temple.

Day 18: The Prophets—Jonah. A ceramic whale.

Day 19: Enslavement—2 Kings 25. Heavy chain links.

Day 20: Daniel and Lions—Daniel 6. A lion.

Day 21: Nehemiah—Nehemiah 2. A clay wall.

Day 22: 400 years of silence—Between testaments. A scroll with a lock glued on it and a moon hanging from it to signify spiritual night.

Day 23: The annunciation—Luke 1. An angel ornament.

Day 24: The birth of Jesus—Luke 2. A picture of a mother and child.

Day 25: The boyhood of Jesus in Egypt—Matthew 2, Luke 2. A pyramid and palm tree.

Day 26: The baptism of Jesus—Luke 3. A dove.

Day 27: The temptation of Jesus—Luke 4. A snake wrapped around a cactus.

Day 28: The first miracle—John 2. Two wedding rings.

Day 29: Feeding the 5,000—Matthew 14. A basket with fish in it.

Day 30: Sermon on the Mount—Matthew 5-7. A miniature lamp.

Day 31: Do not worry—Matthew 6:26-34. A bird.

Day 32: Woman at the well—John 4. A clay well.

Day 33: Raising of Lazarus—John 11. A clay man wrapped in strips of cotton.

Day 34: Palm Sunday—Matthew 21. A palm branch.

Day 35: Cleansing the temple—Mark 11. A whip.

Day 36: Jesus anointed—John 12. A small beaded box.

Day 37: Judas plots—Matthew 26. A bag with silver coins.

Day 38: The Last Supper—Luke 22. A loaf of bread and a cup.

Day 39: Crucifixion—Luke 23. A cross.

Day 40: Mystery Saturday—1 Peter 3:18-22. No ornament.

Day 41: HE IS RISEN!—Mark 16. A clay tomb—empty.

Day 42: The marriage supper of the Lamb—Revelation 19. A place mat with gold silverware.

CHAPTER ELEVEN

HOLY WEEK

April 1982

This Easter has been a revelation. I have never been in a church that celebrates Easter all week long! I love it! We began with Palm Sunday and worked our way through Scripture each day. Monday was the clearing of the temple, Tuesday was teaching in the temple, Wednesday was the anointing at Bethany, Thursday was the Last Supper (called Maundy Thursday), and Friday was the crucifixion.

All of the preparation made this Easter Sunday feel like an explosion. Having lived vicariously through the trial and execution of Christ, the whole church of Christ was singing at the top of their lungs, "He lives, He lives! Christ Jesus lives today!" It was a celebration to remember. One to continue.

More than twelve years have passed since I wrote that journal entry. Celebrations of Holy Week have grown and become sweeter each year. The format changes constantly, but the presence of the Savior stays the same. Whatever the program, whatever the celebration, we are each changed, made new, by the Living Word.

The following is a description of each day of Holy Week and a short story of one of our celebrations to bring the holy home.

PALM SUNDAY

I have always been a fairly capable person. Usually I am able to set my mind on a goal and work carefully and systematically toward it, and I usually succeed.

Weight loss was my Waterloo. I tried every plan on the face of the earth. Okay, that's an exaggeration, but not a big one. I could not lose the fifty extra pounds I carried. I had followed the Astronauts' Diet, Herbalife, Diet Center, Weight Watchers, and several others clipped from magazines.

Enter the Fat Ladies Club. Three friends had found themselves in the same place as I was. They were exhausted with the emotional burden of hating their own bodies. And so God worked in a supernatural way to bring four hurting children together.

Six months later I had lost fifty pounds. Six months of discipline and hard work. Six months of inquiry into the reasons for the weight. Six months of devastating insights.

But once the work was done, a celebration took place. We were celebrating the birth of Jesus and the birth of a new body for Carol. New clothes littered our bedroom, and a glow of satisfaction and happiness surrounded me. Old clothes were given away, and behold! All things had become new!

As we approached Easter that year, it was obvious that something had worked. The weight was staying off. The disciplines of following a twelve-step program were being transferred to other areas of my life that still needed healing. But the cry of need—Step One—had never left me. I remained completely aware of my need for a Savior.

And so, rejoicing and filled with great thanksgiving, we entered church on Palm Sunday. Handed palm branches, we waved them with fervor and cried out corporately, "Hosanna, hosanna. Blessed is He who comes in the name of the Lord." And then the worship leader said these words: "Remember, *hosanna* literally means, 'save us.' The people were crying out for salvation."

Everything in me melted in wonder. "Save us. We need a Savior." Jesus rode into Jerusalem, five days prior to the cross, to the sounds of people begging Him for salvation. "Be our savior," they cried.

And here I also stand. Salvation has visited me. The Savior Himself has heard my cry. I am fifty pounds lighter and years wiser. And yet, on this Palm Sunday, I am so aware of the places in my life that need His saving touch. And so, with shaking hands and tearstained cheeks, I raise my palm and add my cry. "Hosanna! Save us! Hosanna! Be my Savior!"

MONDAY: THE DAY OF TEACHING

On this day Jesus went up to the temple to teach. But what He saw were people buying and selling. In deep anger He overturned the tables of the moneychangers and drove them out, saying, "It is written, My house will be called a house of prayer, but you are making it a den of thieves."

Our bodies are also called temples, temples of the Holy Spirit. They are also to be houses of prayer. So we taught the children about prayer.

And the children, with pure little hearts, bow their heads and make themselves as pure as possible. They pray sweet little prayers and try hard to impress Mom and Dad. Eventually they are sent to bed, and Mark and I are left to smile at their attempts to please.

After all, their prayers were so obvious. They had been told they were to pray, and so they did as they were told. They imitated holiness. They did not understand the concept; they simply did what they knew would please their parents. We laughed quietly, moved to the other room, and both of us went about our own ministries of prayer.

As I knelt, revelation began to course through my veins. I was no different from my small children. I knelt because I had been so taught. I repented because I had been so taught. I praised because I had seen others praise. I requested because I had been taught to bring my concerns to the Father.

Certainly I understood the principle of my body as the temple of the Holy Spirit better than my children did. Or did I? Was I not just imitating my teachers? I thought I had such spiritual maturity, but then so did Noah, Megan, and Rachael.

Had I entered the throne room of God and been the only one unaware of my state? Did the angels see a sweaty little girl with long braids and banged up knees racing toward the Father? Did they witness a little Carol Jo trying so hard to impress the Almighty with her mama's dress-up clothes and her daddy's fine words? Did they see my special offering as the over-glued mess it was?

I thought I had entered as a thirty-three-year-old woman, well dressed and well spoken. I thought I might make an impression.

Instead I am given the blessing of reality: I am no different than my children. Oh, I have a bigger vocabulary and can dress up a bit better. But I am still a bright-eyed, rosy-cheeked child, filled with airs and pretense, anxious to please her heavenly Father.

TUESDAY: THE DAY OF PREPARATION.

> While He was in Bethany, reclining at the table in the home of
> a man known as Simon the Leper, a woman came with an
> alabaster jar of very expensive perfume, made of pure nard.
> She broke the jar and poured the perfume on his head.

Some of those present were saying indignantly to one another, "Why this waste of perfume? It could have been sold for more than a year's wages and the money given to the poor." And they rebuked her harshly.

"Leave her alone," said Jesus. "Why are you bothering her? She has done a beautiful thing to me. The poor you will always have with you, and you can help them any time you want. But you will not always have me. She did what she could. She poured perfume on my body beforehand to prepare for my burial. I tell you the truth, wherever the gospel is preached throughout the world, what she has done will also be told, in memory of her" (Mark 14:3-9).

This story is one I treasure. A woman, caught up in love for the Savior, worships Him in a way others do not understand or condone. He understands and commends.

I always find myself wondering how best to worship. How best to express my love. This year we told the children the story and then built a house out of cardboard. On one side we put a heart with a slit through it. On the other side we put a cross with a slit through it. Each child and adult was given a pad of paper cut in an Easter egg shape. Everyone would leave his or her own love notes to Jesus and other family members in the heart side of the house. The cross side was for notes of repentance.

Then, on the day of preparation, we read the notes as an act of worship. The repentance notes were not read aloud but were prayed over and then burned.

My favorite notes were from the children:

I love you, Jesus.
Jesus, you and me be friends.
Jesus, Rachael gives special hugs.
Jesus, I love baby [Noah's teddy bear]. Do you love baby too?

These are acts of worship, phrased by children. Like the woman in Mark 14, they do not understand the significance of their actions, but Jesus does. And He will keep them.

WEDNESDAY: THE LEAVEN SEARCH

For several years Mark and I had semitraditional Passover dinners on Maundy Thursdays. Because we had never been given the privilege of seeing a real Passover dinner, these came largely from research.

Part of the Jewish tradition surrounding Passover is a leaven search. The Jewish mother does a grand spring cleaning prior to Passover, removing dirt as well as leaven from the house. When every nook and cranny has been cleaned, the father and mother and children take a candle (or a flashlight) and a dustpan and go throughout the entire house making sure all dirt has been removed.

In Scripture leaven is used as a symbol for sin. While a physical search of the house is made, a spiritual search of one's soul is suggested. I love this activity, because it mirrors having one's house clean with having one's spirit clean. Throughout my spring cleaning I ask the Spirit to bring to my mind ways in which I am failing, to bring the dark, damp corners of sin into glorious, purifying light. I always leave the leaven search a mysteriously free person. Each corner has been examined. For three days I have been asking for parables I can understand, and the Spirit has shed light on sin and forgiven it.

One year, after I had conducted a solitary leaven search, I was called on to train a group of image consultants in Idaho. I worked for a company that sells image tools, complete head-to-toe professional dress. That weekend I was to work with one of the top trainers in the nation.

I arrived in Boise, checked into a beautiful hotel, and met the Senior Trainer. The woman was in her late forties, used to having a high salary, used to wielding power, and was abrupt and intimidating. She would be the one to write my review at the end of the weekend, and she let me know she had never written a positive report on anyone. She found Junior Trainers to be unorganized, inefficient, and generally poor teachers. She also told me she would review my personal appearance each day before she let me loose on new recruits. She aimed to intimidate, and I thought she did an admirable job.

The first day passed in agony. I worked harder than I had ever worked before. I taught to the best of my abilities. I was so organized it hurt my head. Still, sour looks were thrown my way.

And so I began to pray. "Lord, I have done all I could to find favor in this woman's eyes. I don't like her, Lord. I think she is hard and unkind. But I would like to keep this training job, so I am asking you to secure me a decent evaluation. Please, Jesus, you must know that I'm in over my head."

After we trained for eleven hours, I was told she and I would dine at a nice restaurant in Boise. Not even my off-hours were to be my own.

We ate at a beautiful Italian restaurant. She talked and I listened. She let me know what she liked and didn't like about the company we worked for. She informed me of my strengths and my shortcomings that day, and I did well not to cry. Then we moved to politics, sex, and religion.

"I can't stand those Jesus people," she exclaimed. "They are so rigid and unbending. They condemn everyone but themselves."

I inhaled sharply and thought, "Oh well, in for a penny, in for a pound."

"Excuse me, I happen to love Jesus dearly. I know His people are often a mess, but could we leave Him out of it?"

Her eyes widened. "Well, I didn't mean to offend. You must know how uneducated and judgmental they are. Not you, of course. I think you are a reasonable person. But honestly, all those protesters outside abortion clinics, all those sleazy TV preachers. You have to agree they don't give your Deity any great reviews."

I welcomed the unseen presence of the Holy Spirit at the table. I was keenly aware that the Spirit had joined us, and I began to enjoy the exchange.

"You're right, of course. His people are often gullible and at the mercy of people who are really wolves. But you can't judge Jesus on the sins of His people. You need to examine who He was and what He taught. The rest is like any other religion, filled with people who keep getting the issues confused."

We both paused. The fettuccine received some honest attention. We both began to smile.

"Do you have a religion?" I asked.

"Of course. I was raised a Jew. I don't keep all the orthodoxy, but I was raised that way."

Before I knew it, I was raving about the aspects of Judaism that I personally love. We talked about the rich symbolism, the history, the celebrations.

And then I said, "You know, because Jesus was a Jew, we do Passover at our house. I don't know if I'm saying this right, but we did a leaven search this year."

"Really! Oh, Carol, I love leaven searches. I used to adore them as a child. In every room Mama left one small item, and we would race to be the one to find the leaven."

She went on with her recollections, and I was treated to a deeper view of Jewish life than I had ever had. After a few minutes she had tears in her eyes and could not go on. My eyes clouded also, and I reached across the table and squeezed this woman's hand. We blinked hard and smiled.

"I hadn't thought of leaven searches in years. I never did them with my daughter. Maybe with a grandchild. Thank you."

The weekend was exhausting, but two daughters of Abraham found common ground for a brief moment. She may never know Jesus as her Messiah. Then again, His name is Savior.

THURSDAY: DAY OF THE LAST SUPPER—PASSOVER

The story of the Last Supper is familiar to all of us. Unfortunately we have lost its historical context. Passover is a miracle of symbolism and prophecy. One year Mark and I were teaching a discipleship class to four young women who had recently graduated from Oregon State University and had asked to be taught. As we approached Holy Week, we decided to do a Passover dinner at our house with these young women and our two babies.

I worked hard to get the research done and the elements of the dinner together. Each person was given a printed program with every reading and response. Megan, two years old, had been taught her all-important line. Everything was finally ready.

The dinner went off without a hitch. Everyone brought the right food. Everyone read at the right time. And when it was time for the youngest person present to run to the door and see if Messiah had come, Megan toddled over to the door and cried, "Messiah has come; He has!"

We shared smiles, loving the voice of an infant proclaiming the arrival of the King. Then we moved to communion, and for some reason the whole thing fell apart. People, familiar with the Eucharist, began to talk among themselves, to tease, to make light conversation. The atmosphere of intense concentration and attention was gone. Here we were, approaching the height of holiness, and people were discussing the start of the baseball season.

I could feel my ire rise. I grew quiet and began to let my eyes wander. This is usually a great technique. Kind of unconscious manipulation. People realize you are quiet and turn their attention back to the program.

Instead they continued, and I became aware of the Lord's presence. The Lord's amused presence. You see, this last supper was very much like the real one. No one really understood the significance of it either. I had asked the Lord to give us a Last Supper experience that was similar to the real one. He had. And I was annoyed.

Realizing the joke was on me, I began to smile. The table quieted, and everyone wanted to know what was funny. I told them. I told them we were just like the disciples, wanting to be with Him and yet not knowing holy ground when we were on it. I told them that this thought, this recognition that we seldom know what we are really doing, would be the theme of my Easter. And then we took the bread and broke it.

FRIDAY: DAY OF THE CROSS—SUFFERING

The family I grew up in saw me as the strong child. Contrary to the truth, sensitivity was never credited to my account. Since I entered the work force, however, each of my employers and my pastors have commented on how terribly sensitive I am. My husband sees it the same way.

Because of this sensitivity, Good Friday has never been one of my favorite days. I can see the scene at the Cross so clearly that it destroys me, even though I am blessed with the knowledge of the coming Sunday morning. Mark and I have learned to be careful in choosing activities for Good Friday. Communion and silent prayer at the Trappist Abbey down the road are wonderful for me.

This last year two of the four of us in the Fat Ladies Club have felt compelled to leave our common church. So two are in and two are out. We approached Good Friday with leaden hearts, hearts filled with lonely despair at our churchless state. The two remaining women suggested that we all have a Good Friday service together. We would meet at John and Wendy's and have a dinner of soup and rolls with all of our families. Then Vicky and Larry would lead worship, I would teach and give the assignment, and we would proceed outdoors for individual acts of worship.

I had been struck all spring by the holes in the hands of Jesus. Holes in His hands. Holes in His feet. A gaping hole in His side. Holes in the one person who was whole. Those holes, those punctures in the Holy One, were made to match the holes in my soul, in my psyche, in my body and spirit. The holes that left me crippled were healed by the holes meant to cripple Him who knew no holes. And so I came to view the cross, not as an instrument of torture, but as an instrument of healing.

Each of us, from the oldest to the youngest (my four-year-old), took a piece of paper and listed our holes. We catalogued those places inside us that knew sin intimately, places where wholeness was not known. And then we left the comfort and beauty of John and Wendy's living room and went out to the carport.

There on the ground was an old, ugly, blood-smeared, eight-foot cross. A crown of thorns desecrated its "head." Large railroad spikes violated the "hands and feet." And there, to the side, was a hammer and a can of nails. In small family groups we took our list of sins, our catalogue of holes, and nailed them to the healing place. Small children nailed easily and seemed completely finished. Adults flinched with the sound and found it less accessible. Yet each of us sought healing in that place, and He who had suffered on those boards came and walked among us, touching this one and that one with hands that bore holes.

Communion followed. The bread and the cup were taken at the foot of that killing device, now littered with slips of sin.

It was a good Friday. A small white sheet of paper bearing the stains of my humanity was left at the cross in the carport. Belonging to the race that yelled "Crucify Him," I am set on a path that leads to life. Set there by the One we crucified. Healed by His wholeness.

SATURDAY: DAY OF MYSTERY AND SILENCE

Scripture reveals little about the three days Jesus was in the tomb. First Peter 3:18 says, "He was put to death in the body but made alive by the Spirit, through whom also he went and preached to the spirits in prison who disobeyed long ago when God waited patiently in the days of Noah while the ark was being built."

Many theologians think this means that Jesus preached to those already dead, reassuring us that no one who has ever lived is out of reach of the grace of God. Whatever we make of that passage of Scripture, all of us agree that the three days remain a mystery. Silence reigns. The disciples are no doubt grieving.

It's fun to take this day and plumb the mysteries of God. Our family tries to think up things about God that we cannot understand and then discuss them. Things like:

If God has always been, who created Him?
Do babies live in heaven first, or does God create them on the spot?
Can God make a rock so big He can't move it?
What does Jesus think of our paint job on the house?

From the ridiculous to the unreachable, we discuss the mysteries of God. It's a day to wonder.

Two years ago I, who consider sewing to be for angelic beings gifted with a patience I can only guess at, took a class on making outdoor banners. The teacher assured us that anyone, no matter how new to sewing, could make these banners. I got the ancient sewing machine out of hiding and went for it.

The class was terrific, and this klutz found she could make a banner. I was amazed at my good fortune; I began to make banners for each month of the year. They hang from our walnut tree and seem to get plenty of attention from passersby.

So far I've made and hung banners that everyone understands: a snowman in January, tumbling hearts in February, a daffodil in March. I've had people stop and ask if I sell them. (This flatters my ego so much that I feel like gathering the children and Mark together and making the people ask again!) Actually, I do not sell them. What takes the average seamstress two hours takes me six. Besides, mine have several unique features I hope no one driving by at thirty miles an hour will see!

For two years our neighborhood has understood my banners. Next April there will be a week few will understand. I plan to make eight banners. Many of them will be somewhat abstract. Palms on Sunday, a whip and overturned tables on Monday, a perfume bottle on Tuesday, a lamb with a list of things to do on Wednesday (preparing for Passover, you know!), the cup and bread on Thursday, the cross on Friday, and on Saturday, the day of mystery, a solid black banner. Sunday's banner will have a dancing woman to signify the women at the tomb and their celebration.

After two years of easy banners, I hope these will cause a few people to slow down their cars and wonder, "What is going on at the Brazos? What does she mean by this one?"

I do not have the gift of evangelism. I feel awkward and uptight speaking to strangers about my Beloved. But I feel bold about my banners! I hope people will have to ask what the banners mean as we enter the holiest week of the year. It is my salute to the day of mystery.

SUNDAY: RESURRECTION DAY!

I was born in 1958 and raised in a world where women were fighting desperately for equality. My schooling was full of admonitions: Be all you can be; recognize no limitations due to sex. Self-actualization and equality of the sexes were the vanguards of my education.

It's not surprising then that the church has always been a place of tension for me. Because of the male hierarchy I have constantly felt inferior, unworthy, distanced from ecclesiastical orders.

Regardless of our views on women in church leadership, all of us can understand how difficult it is to grow up in a church that doesn't fully believe women were equally created in the image of God. In our churches the women that sermons focused on were the temptresses, the Jezebels, the daughters of Eve. While godly women were given some affirmation, it was the Marthas—those who kept the church socials and Sunday schools running—who were applauded. The Marys—those who couldn't quite get enough time at the feet of the Savior—were often suspect. They seemed to be in some way rebellious. Opinionated. Obstinate.

I can remember pastors teaching that God is male. I remember wondering about Mary, the mother of Jesus. All I ever heard about her in my Protestant upbringing was that she was a vessel. What did that mean? Was she for real or some abstract vision shaped like Mom's large flower vase?

I also remember the first time I heard that Jesus loved women. That He came to liberate them. That He saw them as children of God, created in the image of God.

Resurrection Sunday never fails to speak to me of God's affirmation of women. You see, the women were the first to hear those life-changing words, "He is risen!" Women were the ones to go to the tomb. A woman heard the risen Lord's first recorded word, and the first name He spoke was a woman's—"Mary."

Every Easter Sunday I am the first one up. Mark, like the disciples before him, hears those magical words, "He is risen" from the mouth of a woman. The little girls are awakened by their mama's cry of joy, "He is risen!" and they in turn wake up their brother. Those first words belong to women. They are our gift and our heritage. And every year, as I hear women cry out their joy, a place deep inside me, inside the female part of me, is resurrected and brought to nerve-tingling life.

"He is risen! He is risen! Wake up and rejoice!"

Plan carefully for Holy Week. Don't allow it to be jammed with other activities that take your mind off the significance of the week. Meditate on the following Scriptures each day, and watch them change your understanding of Easter.

SUNDAY:

"Hosanna! Blessed is he who comes in the name of the Lord!"
Read Luke 19:28-44 and contemplate the question, Who is this? (Matthew 21:10).

MONDAY:

"Hear, O Israel! The Lord our God, the Lord is one."
Read Mark 12:28-34 and consider this: If your body is the temple (house of the Lord), how are you applying the Great Commandment?

TUESDAY:

"And the house was filled with the fragrance…"
Read Mark 14:3-10 and consider this: Did the woman who anointed Jesus know the full implication? Did Judas know what he was really initiating? Is it not most important to have a "heart" relationship rather than act upon limited facts? What does "anoint" mean?

WEDNESDAY:

A Portrait of Redemption
Read Exodus 12 to prepare your own heart. Through the years, as Jesus ate the Feast of Passover as a young boy or young man, did He realize that one Passover He would be the Lamb of God?

THURSDAY:

"Watch with me."
Read Mark 14:23-26; Matthew 26:36-45; John 17; and Matthew 27:1-31. Let's read these Scriptures with understanding. How amazing that the Son of God allows Himself to be "tried" by His own creation. Imagine yourself as one of the eleven disciples. What emotions would you experience?

FRIDAY:

"Let his blood be on us and on our children!"

These are the last seven statements of Christ as He hung on the cross. Read them and consider who He really is.

1. "Father, forgive them, for they do not know what they are doing" (Luke 23:34).
2. "I tell you the truth, today you will be with me in paradise" (Luke 23:43).
3. "Dear woman, here is your son....here is your mother" (John 19:26, 27).
4. "My God, my God, why have you forsaken me?" (Matthew 27:46).
5. "I am thirsty" (John 19:28).
6. "Father, into your hands I commit my spirit" (Luke 23:46).
7. "It is finished" (John 19:30).

SATURDAY:

"Make the tomb secure!"

Scripture tells us little about this day. Certainly Mary and the disciples were grief-stricken. As for Jesus, 1 Peter 3:18 tells us, "He was put to death in the body but made alive by the Spirit, through whom also he went and preached to the spirits in prison who disobeyed long ago when God waited patiently in the days of Noah while the ark was being built." However puzzling this may be, we can agree with William Barclay: "This probably means that in the time between His death and resurrection, Jesus actually preached the gospel in the abode of the dead to those who in their lifetime had never had the opportunity to hear it. Here is a tremendous thought: The work of Christ is infinite in its range; it means that no man who ever lived is outside the grace of God."

SUNDAY:

"He is risen! Tell the brothers! He is risen!"

Read Matthew 28, Mark 16, Luke 24, and John 20. Think of it! The Lion of the tribe of Judah, the Root of David, has triumphed! Worthy is the Lamb who was slain, to receive power and wealth and wisdom and strength, and honor and glory and praise! Let's see that on this day, this holy Sunday, we celebrate in a manner worthy of Him.

CHAPTER TWELVE

PENTECOST

November 1993

By three o'clock the children were scrubbed, brushed, and clothed. They looked adorable. Kristi hadn't seen them since Noah was a baby, so these three—ages five, six, and seven— would be a surprise for her. Mark had a game to oversee, the state playoffs in soccer. He would join us at the church, and hopefully he would be there in time for the ceremony.

All the way to the church I coached the children on weddings. The girls needed very few reminders. Noah was all questions. Most of them began with "Why?" Not unusual for his gender. Not when large church weddings are the subject. I took it in stride.

"Because they want their friends to see them on this happy day."

"Because it's important to wear special clothes on very important days."

"Because, sweet one, when two people love each other, they like to kiss."

And on it went. Finally the car found the church—a large, imposing structure in the middle of nowhere. I loved it and the huge old evergreens that surrounded it. We looked around for Mark, gave up, and went in.

Before the kids could get too restless, the ceremony began.

"Oh, Mom, she looks like a fairy princess!"

"Mom, her dress is like Cinderella's!"

"I want to be a bride when I grow up."

On the other side of me Noah watched the proceedings carefully. He didn't say much, but the wheels were spinning. Finally, twenty minutes into this cultural no-man's-land, he turned and whispered, "Mom, this is really kinda boring."

I smiled, squeezed his hand, and encouraged him with visions of cake and ice cream afterward. He seemed pacified.

The ceremony continued. It was a long one. Even the girls began to fidget. Finally a closing song. Little bodies strained to see the singers, and excitement filled our small pew as the children heard "A Whole New World" from Aladdin. And there I was, trying desperately to stop them from singing along.

Finally it was over. My sweet friend had married a tall, handsome stranger. My prayers were fun ones. Prayers for specific blessings I desired to be theirs. Prayers that he would be a wonderful husband. Kristi had waited for this man. She did not rush into marriage. I'm optimistic about her chances for a slice of heaven here.

Caught up in my own thoughts, I failed to listen to Noah. His voice rose, clearly heard for several rows. "Mom, you aren't listening. I want to know why anyone would do this?"

Brides and bridegrooms. Agonies and ecstasies. Better or worse. Richer or poorer. Sickness and health. Why indeed?

The emotions of marriage are such that we are often richer when we are financially poorer, better when the worst is occurring, and healthier in some areas while suffering illness. Why would anyone consciously choose the roller coaster experience of marriage? Of two learning to become one?

Noah's question took me by storm. I glanced at the delighted bride and groom and saw his gaze linger on her and her hand reach out for his. They have an amazing awareness of each other, even when they are engaged in separate conversations.

I am anxious to teach my son about marriage, about the price paid and the dividends received. I want him to understand that it is a marvelous mystery. That somehow it is a picture of Christ and His Church. That one day we will enjoy the Marriage Supper of the Lamb, and no one will be bored. And that his role as a bridegroom will teach him volumes about how Jesus feels about His Bride.

Growing up in a tiny Baptist church, I had no clear idea of what Pentecost was. For years I thought it was just the name of the church down the road, the one with the rowdy music. I was in my twenties before I learned to disassociate the word *Pentecost* with a denomination and to relate it to an act of God. In fact, to two acts of God.

Acts 2 gives us the New Testament Pentecost story. Actually, Pentecost was celebrated by the Jewish community as the Feast of First Fruits. First Fruits was the giving of the Law to Moses on Mt. Sinai. Isn't it amazing how God uses symbolism? No action is ever wasted. The law, given to Moses, on tablets of stone. Generations later, the Holy Spirit, given to the Church, on the same day, to write the law upon the tablets of their hearts.

We celebrate Pentecost in two ways at our house. The first is to teach the children that this is the birthday of the Church. It is the day the Bride of Christ was born. And so, because only Mama has been a bride, Mama pulls out all her bridal finery and begins to teach the children the symbolism involved in each piece.

Mark and I had a wonderful courtship and wedding. I wanted to marry him more than life itself. Everything in me knew that we had been created to be together. I never experienced cold feet; rather, flushed cheeks and a rapid pulse. When I read my journal from those days and reflect on my overwhelming desire for Mark, I am constantly aware that those intense emotions are how Jesus feels toward His bride. There is a hunger and a desire for the betrothal period to end and the honeymoon to begin. And so I check my own hunger. Am I as anxious to see my heavenly Bridegroom as I was to see Mark? Do I hunger with the same intensity? When was the last time I cried out my homesickness for Jesus?

The betrothal ring is given to the bride as a mark of her possession. She is betrothed—promised. As Christians the Holy Spirit is our betrothal ring. A beautiful mark of our possession. A token of His promise not to leave us without a comforter. A reminder that He will return for His bride. Because of this, the movings of the Holy Spirit in our lives, however we understand them, are to shine forth and be celebrated.

When my sister was engaged to her beloved, she constantly played with her engagement ring. I would watch her move her hand so the light would shine on the stone. Smiles played around her eyes. She was unaware of anything except that ring as the mark of her loved one.

How often are we caught up in Jesus like that? How often do we cherish the signs of His work in our lives? What kind of a bride are we?

The separation of the bride and groom is viewed by their protective parents as a good thing. A necessary experience. A time of testing.

Mark lived in southern California the last year of our courtship, while I lived in Oregon. I found the separation agonizing. Not only was the mail a poor substitute, we were foolish not to have invested in Ma Bell. Our phone bills were outrageous. And that was in 1983.

But talk about clinging to anything of the beloved's! The letters he sent were read and reread and memorized by accident. We still cherish them. Each phone call was discussed with my girlfriends and analyzed ad nauseam. I was so focused on Mark that I was a pain to be with.

By comparison, the love letters of Jesus are not as dog-eared as Mark's. I have not memorized them all. Oh, there are passages I've loved into my heart and mind. But the intensity, the passion…is it there for my eternal Bridegroom?

I used to daydream about our marriage. It's funny now, but the most poignant and moving picture for me was one of a shared closet, of our clothes hanging side by side. For some reason that picture always brought tears. It seemed so wonderfully permanent.

My eternal Love left with these words, "I am going there to prepare a place for you. And if I go and prepare a place for you, I will come back and take you to be with me that you also may be where I am" (John 14:2-3).

How much time do I spend daydreaming about that place? I earnestly do want Him to return. I hate the separation. And occasionally I catch glimpses of Him, but they are so few. Each visitation makes me hungry for the next one. I want to live in the Bridal Chamber of Jesus. I want my clothes to hang next to His.

White is worn by the bride as a symbol of purity. Virginity is a thing to be highly prized, but how, in this world, do I keep my spirit virginal? How can I be unstained? At that eternal wedding feast I will wear something borrowed— the borrowed robes of my Lover's righteousness.

James tells us that "religion that God our Father accepts as pure and faultless is this: to look after orphans and widows in their distress and to keep oneself from being polluted by the world" (1:27). How often do I visit widows and orphans? How many rooms in my life are unstained by the world?

The veil is worn to keep the bride and groom from knowing each other fully. It is a symbol that they have not yet known fully the marital relationship. We are also veiled. In 1 Corinthians 13:12 it says, "Now we see but a poor reflection…. then we shall see face to face. Now I know in part; then I shall know fully, even as I am fully known."

I am aware of the veil more than any other symbol. I long to see clearly. I desperately want to see, to know as I am known. But for now I wear a veil, a symbol that I have yet to know fully the marriage relationship. I am allowed glimpses, veiled views of my Beloved, but I want to tear off the veil and see Him.

When we die, we are said to pass through the veil. In the ancient Jewish temple an enormous veil kept the Holy of Holies from being clearly seen. Veils remind us that we humans have always known that our vision is clouded, unclear, distorted.

When we study Pentecost this way, Mama's veil is displayed in the living room. A wedding wreath hangs on the wall. Wedding pictures are out, candles lit, and the little girls are on cloud nine. As Noah grows, Mark will begin to teach us his experience as a bridegroom, and the picture will take on new dimensions.

The second way in which we celebrate Pentecost is to examine the actual surroundings of the New Testament experience. This happened by "accident" one Sabbath—one of those coincidences I do not believe in.

It was a Wednesday at 1:30—my usual hour siesta to snooze or read. That day I was reading. In bopped Rachael, age six, fresh from kindergarten.

"Mom, how do you know when you've heard Jesus?" she asked.

"Excuse me, Rachael, what?" I was certain I had heard incorrectly. After all, in the world of dollhouses and Easy to Read books, what child asks how to hear God's voice?

"Mama...." Her tone was condescending. I was sure I was being chastised for not catching the question the first time.

"How do you know when Jesus is talking to you, and how do you know when you are just talking to yourself?"

"Ummmmmm…" I mumbled. I frequently mumble when I'm caught off guard. It buys me time to think. I had the "facts of life" lecture all planned. No one told me there were other questions that were at least as big as sex. No one warned me. Now what?

"Well, Rachael, that's an awfully big question for such a little girl." I paused, hoping for some interaction. Maybe we could discuss her brilliance. Anything but her question. Anything at all to stall.

Silence.

"Honey, Mama doesn't have time to teach you such a big lesson right now. Could it wait until later?"

"Sure, Mom. Why don't you teach all of us on Sabbath?" she grinned. The grin, issued in love, looked strangely challenging. "Great, Rachael. Will do!"

She left the room in high spirits. I, on the other hand, let the book drop from my hands and began to stare off into space. How does a person know she is hearing God? What a question. Well, at least we don't have to teach it today. (Notice how quickly I got from *me* to *we*?) We have till Saturday. Mark is sure to have the inspiration on this one.

Then one last scary thought. If she asks this question at six, what will she be asking at sixteen?

When Mark came home, I shared with him *his* daughter's question. "Don't you think this is for you to teach? I really think she should hear it from you," I concluded.

"Not on your life!" was the response. "She asked her mother. Her *mother* should answer her. It's all yours, sweetheart." With Saturday still two full days away, I shrugged my shoulders and left to make dinner.

Thursday and Friday I spent racking my brain. "First you check everything with the Word," I would mumble. "Then you check with close spiritual friends and mentors. Then you check for peace. Eventually you go with all of that and your gut instinct. And someday, after years and years, you know the Voice." Piece of cake. But how do I teach that to three children ages four, six, and seven?

By Saturday morning I was a wreck. I had no plan, no outline, no story. I couldn't recognize my own mother's voice, let alone the voice of God. The job was beyond me. Impossible.

By Saturday afternoon with the house cleaned and dinner prepared, I was ready to put the impossible into the hands of God. I took my journal, my Bible, and headed off.

After a few hours I began to see how I would teach the lesson—He formed a story in my mind. Yes, I would write Rachael a story, and an hour later it was finished.

It was a sweet story of a little girl who asks her mama how to hear God. Little girls think their mamas know everything, and this little girl was no exception. Her mama told her the question would require a journey. They would start traveling that day, and someday, when she was a very old woman, she would know the whole answer.

Then the mother took the child to visit several adult friends. Each person told the child how they heard God. Grandma heard Him best through the written word. Grandpa heard Him at the ballpark, telling him about rest and play. Ernestine heard Him in the kitchen, reminding her how He loves to feed people. Wendy heard Him in her garden; Daddy heard Him in the mountains. Finally the child asked, "How do you hear God, Mommy?" and the mother knelt down, wrapped the child in her arms, and said, "Oh little one, I hear God in you!" The child responded by saying, "And then I knew that God is every-where, and so is His voice."

With the story complete, I drove to the Abbey and raced into Vespers.

"Drat! I did it again." I had failed to read the schedule. They were celebrat-ing mass. Mass is only celebrated during that time slot on special occasions. Not being Catholic, I am always uncomfortable with mass. I don't know the process and am always self-conscious and afraid of offending someone.

Sighing, I slipped into the back row and tried to concentrate. Suddenly I knew I was on holy ground. They were celebrating mass for Pentecost. Tomor-row would be Pentecost Sunday. In my rushed and crazy life, I had known that this year we would be unable to prepare properly for it. But my heavenly Bridegroom had known my disappointment and had sent a gift. Especially for me. In the form of a story. For Rachael.

That night we told the children about a day when everyone got to hear God in their own language. We talked about wanting to hear Jesus. And I read the children the story of "Rachael's Big Question."

As I tucked the girls into bed, Rachael's hug was extra tight. "Thanks for writing me a story. What does the story mean?"

"Well, honey, remember how each person heard Jesus in different places?"

"Uh huh."

"Jesus has a way of finding out the language of the heart. Then He speaks to you in your heart language."

"Mama, what's my heart language?"

"Rachael, that's the special way you hear the most important things. Don't worry. He will teach it to you."

I kissed her and moved on to Megan's bed.

"Mom," Megan said, "if I come up with a big question, will you write me a story too?"

Holy moments. Holy ground. Given by the Eternal Bridegroom.

1. As you approach Pentecost, reread the story in Acts 2. Then read John 10:1-18. Jesus is the Good Shepherd, and we are to know His voice. Sit down and list the ways God has communicated to you personally.

2. Share this list with your children. Teach them to look for God's work and His voice in their daily life.

3. Study John 14:1-4 and Revelation 19-22. What does it mean to be the bride? Revelation 19:7 says, "Let us rejoice and be glad and give him glory! For the wedding of the Lamb has come, and his bride has made herself ready." What are we doing to make ready?

4. What can you do to help your home reflect this season? The Law is written on our hearts now, not tablets of stone. Can your home reflect the gift of the Holy Spirit? The birth of the Bride of Christ (the Church)?

CHAPTER THIRTEEN

THANKSGIVING

November 1992

Thanksgiving 1992; I am homeless.

Homeless. The word makes me feel like a cheat. Here, in this tiny town in Oregon, there are people without homes. I have a very adequate home. Warm in the winter and cool in the summer. Safe, pretty, and loved. Why cry homeless now?

Past Thanksgivings have included church services where a congregation gathered to give thanks. Those services were always my favorites because they were times when the preaching was set aside and the congregation was offered the chance to give public thanksgiving. Previously childless couples tearfully giving thanks for new children. Singles rejoicing in new spouses. Widows giving thanks for the strength to endure the grieving process.

They were times of laughter and tears. Times of good-byes and hellos. Wonderful times. Intimate times. Holy ground.

This year we are churchless. No, we have not stopped attending; it's just that we are in the process of finding a new church home. We have done this once before as adults. It wasn't fun then, and it's agonizing now. It's agonizing to leave and devastating to stay. We feel compelled to make another trek around Mt. Sinai.

So we visit churches. We enter as orphans, looking for someone who will take us in and love us. Someone who will take the time to bind up some ugly wounds and reaffirm our place in the family of God. Mark requires good preaching. I want an intimate family atmosphere. Both of us are at the feet of the Father asking what He wants.

When I was a child, there was a couple in our church who dressed as Pilgrims every Thanksgiving service. Each year the church had a people's service, and as the opening hymn played, they would walk up to the front pew and take their seats. She would wear a long, gray dress with a white apron and Pilgrim's bonnet. He would have on complete Pilgrim regalia, including pants, a jacket, a hat, a large belt, and buckles on his black boots. I think he even carried an unloaded shotgun.

That couple, while admittedly eccentric, were gems. They reminded us each year that the celebration had historical roots. That real people had some real reasons for giving thanks. That their feast lasted a bit longer than our dinner would. And that their devotion to the voice of God had taken them on an adventure few of us could begin to fathom.

That couple, probably in their seventies back then, were a gift to a twentieth-century church. They were building a memorial to the reality of Thanksgiving in the heart of one small child. They gave flesh and bones to a holiday that had previously been stuck in the pumpkin patch.

That is what this holiday is about. Remembering our heritage. Reclaiming a day that is currently lost to fowl and football. Restoring an altar.

When the Pilgrims left England to find religious freedom, they took a horrible gamble. They were ordinary people, just average families, who heard the call of God and were determined to follow it. They crowded 102 people into the space of a volleyball court and crossed the ocean. They brought the children they loved, with the full knowledge that the Virginia colony had suffered an 80 percent mortality rate. Imagine bringing your loved ones into that type of a circumstance by choice.

They arrived at what is now Plymouth. Although it was an ideal location in many ways, and they were grateful, they lost forty-seven of their community to sickness the first winter.

Then comes my favorite part of the story. Pure magic. Pure Jesus! A fairy tale in history books.

A young Indian named Squanto joined them. Fifteen years earlier he and four other Indians had been captured by Captain George Weymouth and taken to England where they were taught the language. After Squanto spent nine years in England, God moved miraculously to get him passage back to the New World. Upon arriving, Squanto was lured on board another ship in hopes of trading. But the captain took him captive and shipped him off to Spain where he was sold as a slave. Luckily Squanto was purchased by local friars who rescued these unfortunates at the slave blocks. He attached himself to an Englishman and returned to England and eventually gained passage back to the New World. Again.

Squanto arrived six months before the Pilgrims to find his entire tribe dead. No one was left alive. He wandered in grief, without purpose or hope. Eventually he heard of an English colony that was on the verge of extinction because the people were unable to sustain a living.

Squanto took pity on them and arrived to help. Imagine their surprise when they met an Indian who spoke perfect English and who asked for a beer and ate English food. Then imagine their gratitude when he taught them to fish, plant, hunt deer, refine maple syrup, make use of medicinal herbs, and ultimately to make popcorn.

That harvest season the Pilgrims' hearts were flooded with thanksgiving not only to Squanto and the other Indians who helped them, but to God, who had brought them and delivered them. So they invited Massasoit, the Indian chief who had helped them, to celebrate with them. He arrived a day early with ninety of his warriors. Talk about unexpected guests!

Fortunately the Indians brought with them five deer and a dozen turkeys. The feast was such a joy it lasted three days and included wrestling—the forerunner of the NFL.

How often are our hearts so flooded with thanksgiving that our feasts turn into three-day free-for-alls? How often do we party that hard in the name of the Lord? Have we become a somber, ill-humored bunch? These forefathers of ours had something to be ill-humored about. Forty-seven dead. A cruel winter approaching. But they knew how to savor the sacrament of being. They knew how to rejoice in the here and now.

First Thessalonians 5:16-18 tells us to be thankful for everything. That thankfulness is the will of God. When you have lost forty-seven of your nearest and dearest, the only way to retain a thankful heart is to look to the Author of life. When our eyes are trained on Jesus, we find thanksgiving is not an impossibility. Amazingly, it becomes a gift we can give easily and then receive the healing it brings.

This year we will have an Indian doll at our table. Squanto, of course. His story will be told and retold. We will remember his bondage in "Egypt" and the loss of his tribe. We will also remember his gift of life and thanksgiving.

Then we will look at the other ways in which this country of ours has known the mighty hand of God. We will discuss Gettysburg. How the sun reflecting off a bayonet was the difference in one skirmish. How that one skirmish was the difference in the battle. How that one battle was the turning point in the war. How that war was the turning point in our understanding of Thomas Jefferson's prophetic words, "We hold these truths to be self-evident, that all men are created equal and endowed by their Creator with certain unalienable rights."

We will talk about the fog that allowed Washington's army to escape ruin. We will recite the words of Patrick Henry, spoken in a church: "Give me liberty or give me death." We will discuss the women's movement, the civil rights movement, the World Wars, and prayer in the Senate. We'll talk about Christopher Columbus being led by the Spirit of God. About Abraham Lincoln, Benjamin Franklin, Harriet Tubman, Harriet Beecher Stowe, and Paul Revere. A heritage rich with the workings of God.

We'll discuss the good and the bad, the evil and the holy. We won't make excuses, just as the Bible doesn't in telling the stories of David and Bathsheba, of Noah and drink, of Jonah and the "just say no" campaign.

Then we will bow and thank God. For the past work of His Spirit in this vast and wild land. For the continued work of His Spirit in this vast and wild land. And corporately, my small family and I will beg Him to keep His light in this land. To continue to guide us, even through darkness. To keep His eternal flame burning brightly.

1. Begin your Thanksgiving season by reading *The Light and the Glory* by Peter Marshall, Jr. This book gives a wonderful perspective on those who guided our founding fathers and mothers to this land. Then read the letters of Abigail Adams. Read the words of Thomas Jefferson. Read the life of Abraham Lincoln. Watch Jimmy Carter as he and Rosalyn build habitats for humanity. You will not agree with the entire thinking of any of these outstanding individuals. That's not the issue. The issue is that they followed God as they understood Him.

2. Then, as you approach the season, teach your family our nation's history. Teach them the truth of God's work in our land. Teach them the truth of God's work in your family. Thank God for all you have.

3. On November 1 make a list that is five feet long and hang it in the kitchen. Have each family member jot down his or her thanks during the month. Then, on Thanksgiving Day, read them all aloud. And after you have spent three weeks thanking God, beg Him never to allow you to quit being thankful. Beg Him to keep His light in this land and in your home.

Holy Records

✤

*In the future
when your descendants ask their fathers,
"What do these stones mean?" tell them,
"Israel crossed the Jordan on dry ground."
For the LORD your God dried up the
Jordan before you until you
had crossed over. . . .
He did this so that all the peoples
of the earth might know
that the hand of the LORD is powerful
and so that you might
always fear the LORD your God.*

JOSHUA 4:21–24

CHAPTER FOURTEEN

CHRONICLES

I come to this chapter certain of its content. Convicted of and committed to the concept of chronicling. Dedicated to leaving my children with some record of the work of God in the life of their family.

Chronicling is defined as the act of recording historical events in the order in which they happened. This can take many diverse forms. I have friends who chronicle their walks with God in scrapbook form. Others are songwriters who tell of their walks through lyrics. Still others paint a visual story of God's work in their lives.

The Old Testament itself is a chronicle, a chronicle of the nation of Israel commanded by God: "These commandments that I give you today are to be upon your hearts. Impress them on your children. Talk about them when you sit at home and when you walk along the road, when you lie down and when you get up. Tie them as symbols on your hands and bind them to your foreheads. Write them on the doorframes of your houses and on your gates.... Be careful that you do not forget the LORD, who brought you out of Egypt, out of the land of slavery" (Deuteronomy 6:6–12). The nation of Israel was to record His commandments and His workings in their lives so they would never forget that Jehovah had brought them out of Egypt, out of the land of slavery.

I have lived thirty-six years. Plenty of time to know the land of slavery. And plenty of time to have watched my Lord patiently come, lovingly see, and when requested, purchase my freedom. I, too, know Him as Savior.

This knowledge brings with it a tremendous responsibility to teach my children the faithfulness of God in their mother's life, in their father's life, and in the life of our family. In Proverbs 12 we are taught that if we're not diligent, those under our care will give their allegiance to another. These words terrify me. I will give anything to see that my children do not give their allegiance to another. Absolutely anything.

And so I return to Deuteronomy 6. "These are the commands, decrees and laws the LORD your God directed me to teach you to observe in the land that you are crossing the Jordan to possess, so that you, your children and their children after them may fear the LORD your God" (6:1–2).

"Write them—the words of God, the workings of God, the love of God—on your gateposts. Talk about them when you rise up, while you work, and when you rest. Teach them diligently to your children." For this I am responsible.

Ron Mehl, pastor of Beaverton Foursquare Church, says that we may influence many people, but our goal should be to *impact* their lives. Influence is the ability or power to affect others, but impact is a violent contact, a shocking effect. I want my children to have a vivid, shocking, powerful experience with God while they live in my home. I want them forever marked, forever different, forever changed, forever impacted by Jesus. I want my children to be aware of holy ground when they are on it.

Ron Mehl goes on to say that "our task in raising children is not to bring about outward conformity, but inner convictions." I firmly believe this is most likely to happen if we are conscious every single day of the reality of God in our lives and in the lives of our children.

Once again, I turn to the story of Joshua for guidance. After the Israelites miraculously crossed the Jordan River on dry ground en route to the promised land, Joshua instructed twelve men to gather twelve stones and to build an altar as a reminder of what God had just done in their lives. He says, "In the future when your descendants ask their fathers, 'What do these stones mean?' tell them 'Israel crossed the Jordan on dry ground.' For the LORD your God dried up the Jordan before you until you had crossed over. The LORD your God did to the Jordan just what he had done to the Red Sea when he dried it up before us until we had crossed over. He did this so that all the peoples of the earth might know the hand of the LORD is powerful and so that you might always fear the LORD your God" (Joshua 4:21–24). This was a potent memorial to God's power, mercy, and provision.

We also need memorials of God's work in our lives. We need to be keenly aware of His moving and His power. Then we need to record those events so that other strugglers can be reminded that we also struggled. And God answered.

I grew up with such stories of my parents and their walks with God. Like the time Dad had to have surgery on his ear. Although it was painful, if it had gone just a short time longer, the problem would have been unreachable, and personality disorders would have occurred. Now we tease Dad that those disorders had obviously already taken effect, but the teasing is born of wonder at God's timing.

And there was the time in junior high that my friends were headed down paths my parents did not want me to travel. So they put our house on the market, and it sold instantly. A new house, in the high school district where my father taught, was available. Mom and Dad had looked in the area for years and had never found anything, but now, miraculously, a house opened up. We moved, and of those fifteen or twenty junior high friends, only five of us completed high school.

Mark's family has its stories as well. Leo, the new pastor in town, was prowling around the post office after hours trying to mail something. Mark's father, Luke, was the postmaster. When Luke heard someone prowling around, he armed himself with a gun. But instead of a hardened criminal, he found a young pastor with a heart for people. Before long Luke was intensely discipled by that young pastor, and years later that young pastor's wife, Ernestine, would greatly affect the life of Luke's daughter-in-law. Another story of timing. Of provision.

This last year Billy Graham came to Portland. My paternal grandfather had been saved at a Graham crusade in 1950. When I was a little girl, Grandpa would have me sing to him for candy. By the age of five I had learned "Blessed Assurance" and "At Calvary," and to this day, I never hear those hymns without thinking of my dear Finnish grandpa. So one warm autumn evening, Mark and I headed off to hear the Reverend Graham.

Scattered throughout the auditorium were my parents, my sister, my cousins, aunts, and uncles. My grandparents were in the heavenly auditorium, but their presence was felt. As Johnny Cash warmed up the crowd, I saw Mom and Dad. They waved, and we all sat back to enjoy it. Somehow it was more special because we were there together.

Then the crowd was instructed to sing "Blessed Assurance." Tears streamed down my face as Mr. Barrows said this hymn had been the theme song of the crusade in the early days. The words are deeper and truer today than they ever were before.

We left as a group, recalling the story of Grandpa's salvation. How he had turned to Grandma and asked her to go with him at the altar call. How his children and their spouses had followed them up front. How they had wept as their father came to Jesus. How they rejoiced today that Grandpa is with Jesus.

These stories are part of my heritage. They infuse me with a deep and powerful faith in the workings of God. They are family altars, the memorials of God's work in the life of my family.

And so the commandment of Deuteronomy 6 becomes a joy to observe. It is a pleasure to build memorials for the faith of my children, and my home is full of them—the keys, Mama's wedding veil, Daddy's book of Sabbath remembrances. Each is there to honor God and to give Him the glory for what He has done in our lives, in our homes. And they are dedicated with the fervent prayer that someday Megan, Rachael, and Noah will bring the holy home. Home to their own homes.

CHAPTER ONE: HELP!
1. Rainer Maria Rilke, *Letters to a Young Poet* (San Rafael, Ca.: New World Library, 1992), 10.

CHAPTER THREE: HOLY MYSTERY
1. Gerald Tomlinson, *A Treasury of Religious Quotations* (Englewood Cliffs, N. J.: Prentice Hall, 1991), 165.

CHAPTER FIVE: SABBATH
1. Karen Burton Mains, *Making Sunday Special* (Waco, Tx.: Word, 1987), 21.
2. Herman Wouk, *This Is My God* (Boston: Little, Brown & Co., 1959), 45.